# Channel of Peace

# Channel
### of Peace

Stranded in Gander on 9/11

## KEVIN TUERFF

ANANSI

Published in Canada in 2018 and the USA in 2018
by House of Anansi Press Inc.
www.houseofanansi.com

This is a work of nonfiction. The events portrayed are from the author's memory
and personal experiences. While all the stories in this book are true, some names
and identifying details have been changed to protect the privacy of the people
involved.

House of Anansi Press is committed to protecting our natural environment. As
part of our efforts, the interior of this book is printed on paper that contains 100%
post-consumer recycled fibers, is acid-free, and is processed chlorine-free.

22  21  20  19  18        2  3  4  5  6

Library and Archives Canada Cataloguing in Publication

Tuerff, Kevin, author
Channel of peace : stranded in Gander on 9/11 / Kevin Tuerff.

Issued in print and electronic formats.
ISBN 978-1-4870-0513-9 (softcover).—ISBN 978-1-4870-0514-6 (EPUB).—
ISBN 978-1-4870-0515-3 (Kindle)

1. Tuerff, Kevin.  2. Kindness—Case studies.  3. Generosity—Case studies.
4. Social action—Citizen participation—Case studies.  5. Conduct of life—
Case studies.  6. September 11 Terrorist Attacks, 2001—Social aspects—
Case studies.  7. Gander (N.L.)—History—21st century.  I. Title.

BJ1533.K5T84 2018              177'.7              C2017-907399-0
                                 C2017-907400-8

Library of Congress Control Number: 2017961326

Cover design: Alysia Shewchuk
Typesetting: Sara Loos

 Canada Council    Conseil des Arts      ONTARIO ARTS COUNCIL
for the Arts       du Canada                CONSEIL DES ARTS DE L'ONTARIO
                                            an Ontario government agency
                                            un organisme du gouvernement de l'Ontario

*We acknowledge for their financial support of our publishing program
the Canada Council for the Arts, the Ontario Arts Council, and the Government of Canada
through the Canada Book Fund.*

Printed and bound in Canada

This book is dedicated to the people of
Gander, Newfoundland and Labrador.

A portion of proceeds from the sale of this
book will be donated to nonprofit organizations
helping refugees. I hope this book is a reminder that
we promised to "never forget" the lives tragically lost
in America, and the dedication and kindness of first
responders and volunteers on 9/11.

# CONTENTS

*Foreword by Mayor Claude Elliott* . . . . . . . . . . . . . . . . ix
*Prologue: It All Starts with Kindness.* . . . . . . . . . . . . . . . I

CHAPTER 1: Stuck on the Tarmac . . . . . . . . . . . . . . . .5
CHAPTER 2: The Terrible News . . . . . . . . . . . . . . . . 17
CHAPTER 3: Where Am I and Who Are
    These Nice People? . . . . . . . . . . . . . . . . . . . . . .27
CHAPTER 4: We Stink and We Want to Go Home . . 51
CHAPTER 5: Déjà Vu — Back in France . . . . . . . . . . . 61
CHAPTER 6: Pay It Forward 9/11. . . . . . . . . . . . . . . .77
CHAPTER 7: The Return to Gander . . . . . . . . . . . . . .87
CHAPTER 8: Twelve Actors, Twelve Chairs,
    and Two Tables . . . . . . . . . . . . . . . . . . . . . . . . IOI
CHAPTER 9: Kindness and Refugees . . . . . . . . . . . III
CHAPTER 10: No Thanks Are Necessary. . . . . . . . .129

*Appendix: Ten Ways to Pay It Forward.* . . . . . . . . . . . 137
*Acknowledgements* . . . . . . . . . . . . . . . . . . . . . . . . . . . I47

# FOREWORD

ON SEPTEMBER 11, 2001, I was mayor of the Town of Gander, Newfoundland, population 9,000. After thirty-eight transatlantic airline flights carrying 6,500 passengers were diverted here, I declared a state of emergency and asked our residents to help these international travelers. We saw the worst of humanity and the best of humanity, and on the very same day. It was almost too much to absorb as it was happening, but it changed our lives forever.

The author tells his personal story as a stranded airline passenger, along with stories from volunteers who quickly stepped up to help those from more than three dozen countries around the world who needed food, clothing, and shelter. A lot of friendships were developed over five days. We just do good deeds and cherish the memories.

I met Kevin Tuerff in 2011 when he returned to Gander for the tenth-anniversary ceremonies of the 9/11 attacks in America. However, I'd been watching Kevin's Pay It Forward 9/11 initiative since 2002. It was wonderful to see how the actions taken by the residents of Newfoundland inspired him to organize many others to do good deeds for strangers as far away as Texas, year after year.

We never could have imagined our actions would receive so many accolades, including the amazing *Come From Away* Broadway musical, in which the author and I are featured characters. The message of this book is very important because our world is divided, with an increase in hatred and intolerance. *Channel of Peace: Stranded in Gander on 9/11* is a beautiful story about how a seed of love can be planted within someone and years later grow into a beautiful, flowering tree.

I hope that people who read this book will come away with the important message of making kindness part of their daily lives, a choice which can change the world. *Channel of Peace* offers suggestions for how you might make the world better with a simple act of kindness for a stranger.

—Claude Elliott
Mayor, Town of Gander (1996–2017)
Newfoundland and Labrador, Canada

# PROLOGUE

## It All Starts with Kindness

EVERYONE BORN BEFORE 1990 has a 9/11 story. The shocking events of that day changed virtually all our lives in mere minutes and had an immediate and lasting effect on the United States and the world. That morning I was flying home, but my flight was diverted elsewhere, to a place I would have been hard-pressed to name on the map. When I was stranded in an unfamiliar corner of the world, in a tiny, remote town in a foreign country, I was lucky enough to be greeted with remarkable kindness, and that experience restored my faith in humanity. I've been telling this story about kindness ever since.

I was one of the "plane people" whose flight was stranded in Gander, Newfoundland, after thirty-eight planes were rerouted to its isolated airport on the edge

1

of the Atlantic Ocean. Call it charity, call it a relief effort, call it being a good neighbor, the 9,000 residents of Gander did whatever they could to show kindness to the strangers they suddenly found among them—6,579 strangers, to be exact.

The events of that day have become more widely known now thanks to news and documentary coverage and, in recent years, the Tony-Award-winning musical *Come From Away*, now running on Broadway. My personal story is incorporated into the musical—I am the real "Kevin T." The inspiration for this book comes from my involvement with Michael Rubinoff, David Hein, and Irene Sankoff, the creators of *Come From Away*. Like me, they believed that the story of what happened in Gander on 9/11 needed to be told. Their musical catapulted from Sheridan College in Toronto to Broadway's Gerald Schoenfeld Theatre in 2017 thanks to the hard work of producers, cast, band, and crew, and also because there is a powerful message at the core of this story that connects with audiences night after night.

I felt firsthand the power of showing kindness to strangers even when it seemed like the world was falling apart. I was on the receiving end of profound love and acceptance demonstrated in acts as simple as lending an air mattress. People in Gander have a strong sense of interconnectedness: they shovel each other's walkways, share whatever is in the refrigerator, and show hospitality to their own and to "come from aways," their term for anyone who's not from Newfoundland. On September 11th, 2001, they went into overdrive.

People from Gander lead by example, and during those transformational and chaotic days in 2001, they served as a channel of peace. They inspired me to start a campaign called Pay It Forward 9/11 that for over sixteen years, and counting, has helped hundreds of participants engage in random acts of kindness in their communities. (If you're feeling inspired, flip to the back of the book to find out how easy it can be to participate in this kindness initiative on page 137.)

What happened to me in Gander changed my life for the better in every way—personally, professionally, and spiritually. I'm certain that sharing my story, which you now hold in your hands, can do the same for others. I know this because I've been sharing it persistently for over fifteen years. I've heard the reactions of hundreds of people and I've witnessed the growth of a movement of kindness spreading around the world, at a time when our world needs it more than ever.

# CHAPTER 1

_____

## Stuck on the Tarmac

SEPTEMBER 11TH, 2001

I WAS RETURNING to America from vacationing in France when the plane's altitude suddenly dropped and we turned sharply to the north. Our transatlantic flight from Paris was scheduled to arrive midmorning in New York on September 11, 2001. Apparently U.S. airspace was closed and all planes were told to land at the nearest airport. Thirty minutes later, our plane with 272 people aboard would land on an island in the Atlantic Ocean. At the time, I was confused and annoyed by the diversion. But the change in direction proved to be providential.

OUR FAMILY MOVED often when I was growing up, so it's no surprise that I enjoy traveling. My parents, Jim and Julie, were high school sweethearts from Gary, Indiana, who married after my father graduated from college. Soon they moved to Fort Wayne, Indiana, for Dad's first job in the insurance business, and it became my birthplace. Dad's career bounced me from Indiana to Atlanta, to Nashville, to Louisville, and finally — in fifth grade — to Houston. I spent the majority of my childhood with my three brothers in suburban northwest Houston, where I graduated high school. My next move would take me to Austin, Texas, where I studied communications, loved Texas Longhorns football, cofounded a college radio station, and graduated from the University of Texas.

After I graduated, my friends at the University Catholic Center helped me come out of the closet as gay at age twenty-two. One of the priests at my church formed a gay men's support group. It made me feel that I wasn't alone and that my sexual orientation didn't mean I should abandon my Catholic faith. I met several men in the group with whom I have remained friends for more than twenty-five years.

In the early 1990s, our group members were more than members; they became active leaders in the church. Sadly, in 1993, Pope John Paul II wrote a directive to Catholics from the Vatican that proclaimed "the intrinsic evil of the homosexual condition." By the mid-1990s, hope for expanding support groups for gay Catholics to other churches was completely lost. Local bishops and priests were toeing the Vatican line. One day, a young college student who attended my church called home to her conservative parents and told them about our group. Her parents reportedly called the Bishop of Austin. I was told that the Bishop called over to the pastor at my church and immediately squashed the gay support group.

This political action not only broke up a group of friends united by religion but also poked a hole in our faith. Most of my friends abandoned the Catholic Church. I tried to stay involved after the group disbanded, but ultimately I stopped attending Mass.

The energy I put into my faith and my local church was shifted into starting a company that promoted good. In 1997, I cofounded and led America's first marketing agency focused solely on improving public health and the environment. Starting a new business was scary and exhausting because of the pressure to continually keep new clients coming in the door, so that employees would always have food on the table with a monthly paycheck. I didn't have time for volunteering with charities, or connecting with friends and neighbors. I worked seven days a week. It paid off. Our firm won the "Don't Mess with Texas" litter prevention campaign with a staff of four, beating out national ad agencies. I wanted to prove that I could be good at doing good, despite what church leaders or others in society thought of me because of my sexual orientation.

By 2001, I decided it was time to take a much-needed vacation, so my longtime partner Evan and I went to Europe. We were returning home after having had a great time, except for Air France losing our luggage for the first two days of our trip. We went to the store and bought cheap T-shirts. We spent our time discovering the South of France, Amsterdam, and Brussels. On our last day, we took the bullet train from Brussels to Paris, staying the final night at a nice hotel near Charles de Gaulle Airport.

Our flight left early on the morning of September 11, 2001, so we decided to spend a few hours in Paris with a taxi driver serving as our personal tour guide. I had a new Sony MiniDV camera, so I was taking a lot of video throughout our trip. We drove by most of the major monuments, getting out of the car to walk up to some of them. I narrated as we walked, "Here we are, walking toward the Eiffel Tower on September 10th, I believe."

Late the next morning, we transferred from the airport hotel to Charles de Gaulle Airport. The security at the Paris airport was more attentive than at American airports. I understood that stricter security in France was a result of several airport terrorist attacks in recent years, so this didn't bother me. Security officials with guard dogs stopped us and asked us questions before we could check in at the Air France ticket counter. Air France Flight 004 would fly from Paris to New York. From there, we would transfer to Continental Airlines and fly home to Austin, Texas.

Evan's favorite cocktail was vodka with club soda. His favorite vodka was Grey Goose, which says "Product of France" right on the label. Throughout our vacation in France, Evan tried in vain to order a Grey Goose cocktail. It took us a while to realize that the French only drink wine. We wondered if Grey Goose was truly made in France. Then, as we were about to depart Paris, Evan stepped into a duty-free shop inside the airport. He emerged with a big grin on his face and two large bottles of Grey Goose.

As we waited at the gate, our passports were checked repeatedly, and eventually we were allowed to board. Back then, economy class actually had decent meals on international flights. We were served shrimp salad with melon and mint, chicken with Poitou-style sauce and rice, Rondelé cheese, and Charente-style tartlets with wine. They also served free liquor. I ordered a gin and tonic. The flight was smooth and easy. I had never seen the movie *Shrek*, and the airline played it on an overhead TV if you purchased a headset. I bought one and settled in for a pleasant two-hour diversion during what I assumed would be an otherwise dull and unremarkable flight.

AIR FRANCE FLIGHT 004 was due into New York at Newark Liberty International Airport around 11 a.m. The United States is roughly west of France, but at one point after the movie, I looked up at the TV monitor and noticed on the live GPS map that our plane had changed direction from west to north. It looked like we were flying to the North Pole. I wondered, *Maybe the GPS has gone haywire?*

Several minutes later our Air France pilot, Captain Hollande, came on the public address system and said something in French. I recognized two English words: "terrorist activity." I looked up at the GPS screen, but the map was flashing back and forth between English and French. The French translation for the Canadian province of Newfoundland is *Terre-Neuve.* I recognized this word on the screen, but I wasn't quite putting it together yet.

*Okay, we're flying a weird route over Terre-Neuve,* I thought. Then the captain came on the PA, in broken English, saying, "Due to a terrorist attack in the United States, we will be landing in Gander."

*Huh? Where are we landing, and why? Did he say—?*

I turned to Evan and asked him if he had heard what the captain said. He hadn't been paying attention. We were enjoying free drinks as we flew across the Atlantic, so what was happening didn't immediately sink in. When a flight attendant walked briskly by and told us to put our tray tables up for landing in Gander, it was time to sober up.

I later found out from fellow passenger Sue Riccardelli, who was flying home to New Jersey, that after the announcement she saw her flight attendant say something to another flight attendant who then looked as though she might faint.

Before I knew it, we were low enough to see land. I took out my camera and snapped a photo. Outside the window were huge green trees as far as I could see. There were no signs of civilization until we bumped onto the runway and cruised to a stop.

We waited in our seats and the plane waited on the tarmac. We were told we would be stopping for quite a while and perhaps diverting to Montreal or Toronto later in the day. We received no specific news about what had caused our diversion beyond what the captain had said earlier. So we sat patiently as the flight attendants continued to ply us with free drinks.

Gander International Airport is a small commercial airport that used to serve as a British air force base during World War II, which is why its capacity is much larger than one might expect to service the small town of only nine thousand residents. When it was built, almost all transatlantic planes needed to stop there temporarily for refueling because of its location on the island of Newfoundland, the easternmost tip of North America. Later, innovations with large jets would allow larger fuel tanks to fly farther. During World War II, the U.S. military paid Canada to expand their facilities to accommodate air force planes making trips to Europe.

Gander airport has seen its share of famous passengers, including the Queen of England, but its strategic positioning has also caused some problems. Once a plane traveling from Russia to Cuba landed in Gander and crew allowed passengers to stretch their legs in the terminal. Before long some Russians had jumped the fence in an effort to escape from communism by claiming political asylum in Canada.

The resource-rich and militarily strategic island of Newfoundland has always had unique relationships with Britain, Canada and the United States. It was once under British dominion, alongside Canada, Australia and New Zealand. Canada became a sovereign country in 1867 and in 1949, Newfoundland joined confederation with Canada as a province (albeit through a referenda process which many Newfoundlanders find dubious). Today it is one of Canada's ten provinces and its official name is Newfoundland and Labrador.

I didn't know all this in 2001, but I did notice that Gander airport had an unusually long runway. I had little else to do while waiting in my seat but glance out the window over the wing. By noon there were dozens of wide-body aircraft landing behind us, one after another. I noticed familiar planes — the red and blue of Delta, American, and Continental — and unfamiliar ones — El Al, Lufthansa, and the green shamrock of Aer

Lingus. Soon Royal Canadian Mounted Police (RCMP) officers stationed themselves on the tarmac, one below the cockpit of each plane. These Mounties weren't like what I expected: they weren't on horses and didn't wear red jackets. Each carried an automatic rifle. *Is it possible there's a hijacker or a bomb on our plane, or maybe on the runway in Gander?*

Over the course of the day, thirty-eight jets (mostly wide-body planes) landed at Gander, causing quite a challenge for local air traffic controllers. These thirty-eight were a part of the 122 East Coast planes diverted from the North Atlantic to Newfoundland and the Maritime provinces in Canada. The Gander International Airport generally saw fewer than a dozen small commercial planes daily. There were no Jetways (walkways from plane to terminal) at the Gander airport. Instead they had a few trucks that drove stairways up to aircraft for deplaning onto the tarmac.

The passengers on our Air France plane were waiting patiently for the most part, but it was slowly becoming clear we weren't going anywhere. No truck with a stairway was pulling up to the side of our plane. Evan and I would stand and walk up and down the aisles of the aircraft. Other passengers generally stayed quiet in their seats.

Five hours after we landed, the captain came over the PA system again. This time, he provided what little information he had. "What we know now is that two aircraft were hijacked and flown into the World Trade Center. Both towers have fallen. The Pentagon was also attacked by a hijacked aircraft."

There were gasps from several passengers. I felt my heart leap into my throat.

Evan was smart and knew his history. "That's impossible," he said. "In 1945, someone flew a B-25 airplane into the Empire State Building and the building survived just fine. The twin towers can't fall."

"Who could make that up?" I said.

We didn't understand that the planes were jumbo jets recently loaded with tons of gallons of fuel for cross-country flights. The fuel had turned each one into a giant bomb. Evan was always a skeptic. I tended to trust authorities.

*Could it be true?*

My mind was spinning, trying to imagine all the chaos in New York City and Washington, D.C. How many people were killed on the airplanes? How many others were killed and wounded? Was it a surprise attack like Pearl Harbor, and if it was, who did it? Was our military elevating our threat level? Were missile silos being opened up, ready to aim and fire? Or was the Pentagon rendered useless by this attack? Were attacks taking place in several countries or just in the United States? How long would this go on? Were we sure our plane didn't have a hijacker on it?

I looked out my window at another plane landing and prayed an "Our Father." Praying helped. I soon felt calm, even safe, on our plane, even though I didn't have any reason to believe it was free of terrorists. I sensed we'd be okay in Gander.

# CHAPTER 2

---

## The Terrible News

SEPTEMBER 11TH, 2001

AS ANXIOUS AS we were, Evan and I and many other passengers couldn't see live TV images, hear radio, read a website, or even call anyone to verify the news we'd been told. It was clear there was a crisis in the United States, but without seeing TV or reading anything, it was difficult to imagine.

The idea of airplanes purposefully crashing into buildings seemed absurd. I couldn't picture it in my mind. I wondered if there were additional planes headed for landmark buildings across the country.

Around 3 p.m., a woman seated in the row behind us was starting to have an argument with her husband.

After five hours on the tarmac, she wanted off the plane and wouldn't accept that we weren't being told more details about what was happening in America and whether or not we were going home. She wanted a phone to call her young children, but that wasn't happening. Her agitation grew louder.

Her husband tried to quiet her, but that only made her cry harder. Everyone around her could hear her anxiety and frustration. Evan turned around and asked if she needed some medication to ease her nerves. (They both declined.)

Evan and I agreed that our friends and family would be worried because we were scheduled to fly into New York City that morning. My flip phone was useless for international calls. The only passengers successfully placing outside calls were sitting in first class. Their seats came with satellite phones activated by credit card. After hours of hearing a few uninformative updates from the captain, I walked up to first class and found a man with an empty seat next to him. He was happy to let me sit there and use the phone. I tried calling my parents in Nashville. I also tried calling my office in Austin. No luck: the calls never even connected. I tried calling friends in other time zones. As I swiped my credit card over and over again, all I kept hearing was the message "All circuits are busy." I returned to my seat.

Later, I would learn that virtually everyone in America was calling everyone they knew to make sure they were okay. The country's phone system was overwhelmed.

Around 5 p.m., I took out my frustration by journaling on the Air France flight menu:

> The world changed today, for the worse. Our flight from Paris to New York missed an international terrorist disaster in New York and Washington, D.C. (Hijacked planes crashed into WTC & Pentagon.)
>
> We've been sitting on our plane now for 12 hours (7 now on the ground). All we can do is wait patiently for news about the tragedy, for a place to try to talk to our families. We've been told we may have to sleep here overnight (on board). We are fortunate to be alive. Many on the plane cried when we heard the news. Everyone is shell-shocked.
>
> No one can imagine what is next regarding our national security. Who can we trust now? Will this heinous crime start a war? All I can do is pray.
>
> P.S. Just learned we will soon depart plane and perhaps spend night in a school here. At least 30 planes here waiting with stranded passengers aboard.

Around 6:30 p.m. in Gander, it was getting dark outside my window. I walked back up to first class with the idea of calling Europe, instead of the United States. It worked! The call connected and I reached my high school friend Todd, who lived in Amsterdam, where it was around 11 p.m. local time. We had just visited Todd a few days before on our vacation. Earlier that afternoon Todd had been walking around Amsterdam with a friend from New York when they heard about the attacks. They decided to go to her house to watch the news. When I reached him, I asked, "Is it true what they're saying?"

"It's horrible," he replied. "I'm watching it live on TV now." Todd explained that terrorists had hijacked the planes and ultimately destroyed both towers of the World Trade Center, killing thousands. Another plane crashed into the Pentagon, and yet another—which may have been headed to the White House or the Capitol—crashed into a field in Pennsylvania. Early estimates of the dead were nearly ten thousand. Tears welled up in my eyes. We didn't know about the plane in Pennsylvania. I was more scared than I could remember, and so was Todd.

I told Todd how I was stuck on the airplane and I couldn't reach anyone in America to let them know I was safe. I asked him to try to call my parents in Nashville and my office in Austin. I also gave him the names and phone number of Evan's parents.

I returned to my seat in coach. Sharing whatever scraps of news I could, however terrible, was the least I could do for my fellow passengers. After all, we were all in this together. Standing up, I spoke to a few people in the row behind me, and soon, dozens of passengers seated within earshot were glued to my every word. Getting confirmation that what we had heard from the French pilot was true brought on a deep sense of grief around us. Nobody asked for more details because they could tell I didn't have anything more.

There were passengers on our plane from more than twenty-five countries. Everyone seemed to be getting along well despite the different languages and cultures represented by the international melting pot of passengers.

Everyone wondered if they might know someone who had been harmed. We felt horrible for the family and friends of the people on those four domestic flights, not to mention the workers and first responders in the World Trade Center and Pentagon. Months later, we would learn that 2,996 people were killed and more than 6,000 injured.

IT HAD BEEN an interminably long time since we boarded the plane in Paris. The crew tried their best to reassure anxious passengers by giving out more free liquor and playing and replaying movies on the overhead TV (instead of the GPS screen). For every hour that went by, we got another free drink. Meanwhile someone hit rewind to play *Shrek* for another, agonizing time. It felt strange to laugh at jokes in a movie while New York and Washington were burning. I felt helpless.

I wanted to help my fellow Americans, or reach out and talk to friends and family. "Hallelujah," the Leonard Cohen song from the movie, kept repeating in my mind in Rufus Wainwright's beautiful voice.

Meanwhile, the lack of communication was causing my family stress.

If I had been at home in Austin, I would have certainly been at the office, glued to the television. At my company in Austin, there was a lot of anxiety. Both company principals were traveling that day, one returning from a trip to the U.S. Open in New York City, and me, returning from Europe through New York. Sara Beechner, the manager on duty, was getting ready for work when her fiancé called her into the living room to watch the attacks on live TV. She recalls, "I remember the optimist in me thought, 'What a horrible accident. How could someone accidentally crash a plane into the tower?' I just couldn't compute it to be terrorism. I didn't understand the gravity of the situation. I had to get into the office."

Valerie Salinas-Davis, the other company principal, landed safely in Austin. She had been on one of the last planes to leave New York before the attacks, and one of the last in the air before the airspace was shut down. Sara later told me, "We got word Valerie was safe, so we were just trying to figure out, 'Where in the hell is Kevin Tuerff?'"

Staff were in shock because news reports were saying that other planes in the air all across the country could be potential missiles, and there was no way I could reassure them that I was okay.

My older brother Brian, from Austin, had gone on a Gulf Coast fishing trip with friends in South Texas that day. His boat had headed out before the attacks began, so he didn't know about the tragedy unfolding. His wife Jana knew I was flying back from Paris, so she called my father in Nashville.

When my dad answered the phone, Jana said, "Please tell me Kevin is okay." Dad paused, somewhat choked up, and said, "I can't tell you that yet."

Jana desperately tried to reach her husband about me but could only reach the marina manager. She told the manager to let Brian know as soon as he returned what was happening and that I was okay. When Brian's boat arrived late that afternoon, the marina manager anxiously greeted my brother and got the story backward. He told Brian, "There was a terrorist attack. Your brother was on a plane. Planes crashed into the World Trade Center. But he's okay."

Brian freaked out, thinking I'd been killed during my flight, but before too long he reached Jana by phone and she clarified that I was safe in Canada. By that time, all flights had been canceled, so Brian and his friends rented the last car in South Texas and drove straight home to Austin, arriving five hours later.

Thankfully, my friend Todd was successful at contacting my friend and colleague Sara in Austin and letting her know Evan and I were safe in Gander. Sara took it from there, calling both sets of our parents. They were relieved to know we were okay, even after they had seen the flight updates online, thanks to my brother Greg who found out on the Air France website that my flight had landed safely in Newfoundland. They had to look on a map to see where that was in Canada.

I meanwhile was still sitting in my tiny airplane seat. It had been more than seventeen hours since we'd first boarded the plane: eleven hours since we landed in Gander, plus the six more spent in travel from Paris. I really wanted off that plane — I was desperate for some fresh air — but I had to admit that I was also nervous about what we were going to encounter when we rejoined the world outside of that bubble. The news as we understood it was terrible, but what if it got worse? Was America at war and if so, were we safe in Canada? Would a gay couple be welcomed in this rural small town? There was an unmistakably awful feeling that the world had changed, but I didn't understand how.

I said another "Our Father" prayer, smiling to myself at how easily the words came to my lips. I learned to pray the "Our Father" and other prayers from my Catholic parents and by attending Catholic elementary school. In second grade at St. Henry's Catholic school in Nashville, Tennessee, I remember thinking that the only way to heaven was for me to become a priest. So one day, when I thought my family wasn't around, I set up an "altar" in the family dining room made of cardboard boxes and bedsheets borrowed from the linen closet and started pretending to consecrate the Communion. And then my mother walked in and asked what I was doing. I was embarrassed! I grabbed my make-believe chalice and ran into my bedroom. Mom was far from angry—she started telling her friends that I wanted to become a priest when I grew up.

I knew I wasn't the only passenger who had serious thoughts in mind, but I was trying outwardly to keep things light and be agreeable, despite the stress.

Finally, our captain announced that we were deplaning. He had no information about where we would be going except that it was to a shelter. We could not take our luggage, only our carry-on bags. Authorities were fine with screening passengers, but there was fear that luggage might contain bombs.

*Were we going to a refugee camp with tents and cots? Should we take pillows and blankets?* I wondered. Unsure of what we were in for in this tiny town of Gander, Evan and I spotted and swiped a full, sealed bottle of Evian water from the flight attendant cart as we left. In our carry-on bags, we had three cameras, two passports, and two sorely needed bottles of vodka.

# CHAPTER 3

---

## Where Am I and Who Are These Nice People?

SEPTEMBER 11TH AND 12TH, 2001

AFTER FINALLY STEPPING off the plane, walking down the stairway onto the tarmac, I felt a great sense of relief. It was around 9 p.m. It was dark and the air temperature felt cool—I wished I wasn't wearing shorts. I turned on my video camera and captured the airport's "Gander" sign. I spoke into the microphone, "We're free, we're free! After I-don't-know-how-many hours on that awful plane, we're free. We don't know where we're going, but we're going."

I turned the camera to Evan. He said, "We're in Gander, and all I know is they'd better have CNN here."

Inside the airport, security was very serious and tight, and there were just two Canadian immigration and customs authorities available to check passports. The airport staff would work around the clock nonstop for days to deplane the over six thousand stranded passengers.

We were among the first. After the immigration screening, we entered the main terminal, which was barely bigger than a high school auditorium. And that's when the first wave of unconditional love hit us: the terminal was filled with volunteers greeting us as we registered. It was like we had walked into a party! There were dozens of volunteers present. Some were wearing their Salvation Army or Red Cross uniforms and sat at ten-foot-long tables. Their job was to make sure every stranded passenger was documented and taken care of. Most of them were older adults, perhaps looking a bit Irish, like me. There were dozens of volunteers at tables set up with food that had everything from home-baked cookies and squares to buckets of KFC fried chicken.

The Air France flight crew had distributed all the food they had, so we weren't hungry. Thinking we might be headed to a tent camp, Evan and I grabbed lots of food and drinks, unsure of when we might be fortunate enough to have these items again. We were told to head outside immediately to a waiting school bus that would drive us to our shelter.

Just then, I spotted a pay phone (remember those?) inside the terminal. I grabbed it and made an international collect call to my parents in Nashville. I knew they'd be sitting nervously by the phone waiting to hear from me.

I heard the operator dial the number, and then I heard my mom's voice say, "Hello?" The operator said, "I have an international collect call from Kevin, will you accept the charges?" She did.

"Hello?" I said.

Dad picked up another phone at home so he could join in. "It's so great to hear your voice," he said.

When I heard their voices, I immediately started to cry.

Mom also choked up but said, "It's okay, it's okay to cry."

"I'm in Iceland or Nova Scotia," I said, confusing the details all over again amid the flood of unexpected relief.

My dad quickly said, "No, we've been tracking you. We know where you are. You're in Gander."

"Is that in Iceland?" I asked.

"No, you're on an island called Newfoundland in Canada." My dad pronounced it *New-found-land*. I would soon find out it's pronounced *Newfinland*.

"What in the hell is going on?" I asked. "We haven't seen any TV."

"Four planes were hijacked and crashed into buildings, exploding like bombs. New York and Washington are in complete chaos," Dad replied. "It's unbelievable."

Almost as soon as I began talking to my parents, a local volunteer told me I needed to hang up the phone or I would miss my bus to the shelter.

"Mom, Dad, I have to go," I said. "I love you."

As soon as I hung up the phone, the volunteers must have realized they would never get the passengers off the planes promptly if everyone tried to call home from these pay phones. As Evan and I moved along, I saw them tape a fake sign on the phones that said "out of order." I felt bad for the passengers behind me in line. For some, it would be another twenty-four hours or more before they could deplane in Canada.

We loaded onto the school bus and off we went into the darkness.

THE TOWN OF GANDER managed a massive volunteer effort in a matter of a few hours. At midday, the town council declared a state of emergency and Mayor Claude Elliott went on local TV and radio to urge everyone in this town of 9,000 to help out their unexpected 6,500 guests.

The people of Gander heeded Mayor Elliott, though most had decided to do something before they'd even heard the mayor's call to action.

Diane Davis, a teacher at Gander Academy, remembers driving down to see the planes at the airport that afternoon. She recalls, "Traffic was bumper to bumper past the end of one runway. Police directed cars of curious locals past. Planes, huge passenger planes, were nose to tail or side by side, with some of their wing tips overlapping. Some planes had open doors, which indicated the passengers were still aboard, with police cruisers circling the taxiways."

After seeing the magnitude of the situation, Diane thought she could do something, so she went to the town hall to volunteer. Soon, she'd be co-managing a school-turned-shelter with more than seven hundred people sleeping on the floors.

The power company sent employees to pick up groceries to distribute to schools that were turning into refugee shelters. The company paid for all the expenses.

And that was just the start.

At 7 p.m., Nellie Moss and her husband, Mac, were at home watching the news when he got the call from the town emergency operations center that 272 airline passengers would be sent to the College of the North Atlantic, across the street from the power company where Nellie worked. Mac was the top administrator at the college.

Nellie remembers: "Mac told me, 'Well, we have to look for bedding, pillows, whatever.'" So she called her friends, and they called their friends, and then their friends did the same, creating a snowball effect. "In an hour or less, I had my car filled with bedding and I was on my way to the college. I remember taking everything in my house—everything except what was on my bed."

After he got a call from the Gander Emergency communications center that he should expect all the stranded Air France passengers to arrive to his college in just ninety minutes, a somewhat panicked but exceptionally capable Mac Moss called on his team leaders. He recalls his instructions to the volunteers that night:

Team 1, Commercial Cooking—Go immediately to the grocery stores and gather up enough food, water, cereal, fruit, juice, snack food, and energy bars to get us through the night, morning breakfast, and lunch tomorrow. Get enough food for three hundred people! Team 2, Electronics—Start stringing cable to set up two TVs in the cafeteria. Set up a microphone for a PA system. Team 3— Gut out the cafeteria of all non-essential furniture and set up tables and chairs for the arriving guests, plus another line for tea and snacks. Teams 4 and 5—Find all available classrooms, stack desks and chairs, sweep the floors, and make the space ready for sleeping areas. Team 6, Registration—Set up tables at the front entrance to intercept the passengers and gather names, addresses, etc. Call the radio stations to announce that the campus will be closed to students until further notice. Team 7, Nursing—Intercept passengers on arrival and see if anyone immediately needs medication for diabetes, blood pressure, etc., or if anyone is in medical distress.

Reflecting back on those marathon days, he added, "We had 148 volunteers at the college, and we were all busy."

Before long, thanks to the work of people like Nellie, Mac, and Diane, all public buildings, churches, and schools in Gander had been converted to shelters. Gander's three hotels were emptied out so that the airline pilots and crew from the thirty-eight planes could stay there to rest. Supermarkets and fast-food restaurants donated all the food they could, and no one asked who was paying the bill.

THE RIDE FROM the airport to the college was less than fifteen minutes, but it felt much longer. The driver of our school bus told the passengers he was taking us to the Gander campus of the College of the North Atlantic. He spoke with a thick accent that sounded like we had landed in Ireland, not Canada.

Evan and I watched out the window, although there wasn't much to see through the darkness along the Trans-Canada Highway except for miles of trees. Once the driver announced our destination, he gave no further commentary about where we were nor information about what to expect when we got there. It might have been helpful to know Gander had a Walmart, Subway, and KFC, all of which we discovered later. It was a tiny town, but it was hardly a third-world country.

After getting off the school bus around 9:30 p.m., we walked through the dark up to the doors of the community college. There were no students—only the exhausted passengers from the Air France flight and dozens of local volunteers, who funneled us into the cafeteria, where they had plenty of food and drinks, plus what we really wanted: TV news. At one end of the cafeteria was a TV tuned to a French-language news network, and at the other end was a TV tuned to CNN in English.

The Salvation Army and Red Cross did an amazing job that first night. Within an hour of our arrival, the Salvation Army showed up with a Ziploc bag for each passenger, containing a feminine sanitary napkin, a toothbrush, and toothpaste. Residents stopped by the college with donations of food and bedding continually throughout the night. It was like we had landed at a free buffet with cod au gratin (fish and cheese casserole), doughnuts, hot dogs, soft drinks, and more.

The college had three nurses on staff, who intercepted passengers as they checked in to identify whether anyone had medical needs. There were a lot of diabetics and people with high blood pressure. They had all their medications in their checked bags, which had to be left on the plane. If a passenger had an issue, the nurses went to local pharmacists, who were also working around the clock, and brought back everything requested. Passengers asked how much they should pay but were told it was free.

Around midnight, I spotted a teenage boy walking through the front door carrying a double-sized air mattress and two pillows. I was bone tired and I knew falling asleep on that air mattress would feel so much better than on the tile floor. I nearly ran over to meet him.

Until that time, I had never been in a situation in my life where I needed a hand from a stranger. It wasn't that I couldn't afford a hotel room—there were no rooms. I was always a problem solver, but at this moment, I had to rely on the kindness of strangers to help me with my basic needs. In the Bible it's written, "For I was hungry and you gave me food, I was thirsty and you gave me drink, I was a stranger and you welcomed me" (Matthew 25:35). This welcome was happening. The people of Gander seemed to need little encouragement.

As the teenager handed me his bedding, a lump of gratitude rose in my throat. I said, "Thank you."

"No problem, b'y," the young man said in his accent before turning and walking back out the door.

I was tired, so, having secured comfortable bedding, I went to find Evan, but he wasn't ready for sleep. He was glued to the cafeteria TV, surrounded by other passengers, watching the images of the planes hitting the World Trade Center again and again. By this time, it was clear that thousands of people, including many first responders, had been killed. We were in shock, coming to understand later than the rest of the world what had happened on this horrific day.

We comforted ourselves with the buffet line in the cafeteria. At one point, I turned on the camera to capture Evan chomping on a hot dog with mustard oozing out of it. I jokingly (and incorrectly stating our location) said to the camera, "Wow, we had to come all the way to Nova Scotia to get a hot dog."

But we were shaken. Underneath our laughter, our nerves were on edge. So we turned to other comfort: our stash of Grey Goose vodka.

I commandeered a space in a classroom and set up the mattress. I wondered how the volunteers and other passengers would feel about two men sleeping together on the same air mattress. While Evan and I had been out of the closet for several years, I didn't know what to expect in a small town in another country. We finally went to sleep around 2:30 a.m. The wonderful air mattress had a leak in it, so soon after lying on it, we heard the air flowing out until we lay on the cold tile floor and pulled the sheet across ourselves. Shortly thereafter, someone in the room vomited, perhaps from all the free booze on the airplane. The stench was awful, so we hauled our air mattress, sheets, and pillows to another classroom.

As we settled in to sleep again, I was happy Evan was with me on this trip. It was exhausting and scary, and being a solo traveler would've been hard.

WHILE EVAN AND I slept, the town of Gander was on the move. Unbeknownst to me, thousands of Gander residents were working to help us. Many, including Mayor Elliott, went without sleep for several days. At times, it seemed like all nine thousand men, women, and children in town were volunteering in some capacity at one or all of the several shelters set up for the "plane people."

High school media teacher and part-time Rogers TV reporter Brian Mosher logged twenty-seven straight hours helping passengers by cooking breakfast at Gander Collegiate, the local high school. Just as he was trying to go to bed at 9 a.m. on September 12th, he was called back to the TV station. He went on the air immediately, playing a key role in conveying to locals what the needs were at each of the different shelters. Brian was amazed by how quickly people responded to specific requests for food, toiletries, and clothing. He worked three live shows per day for the next four days, running back and forth between the school and the station. "Sleep was basically short catnaps, and there weren't many of those," he said.

Retail clerks and pharmacists worked around the clock. Telephone company workers set up temporary phone banks. Everyone with a kitchen started cooking.

After Gander was filled to capacity with refugees, the even smaller towns nearby like Gambo, Lewisporte, and Appleton stepped up to help. Local bus drivers who were on strike left the picket lines to help transport passengers thirty miles or more each way during the emergency.

Mac and Nellie Moss lived one house down from Nellie's sister Sue and her husband, Ron Walsh, who were also a part of the volunteer effort. Sue was the first to bundle her bedding into Nellie's car. Years later Sue would tell me, "We wrote our names on our pillows, hoping we'd get them back after this was over." After all the refugees had left, Sue Walsh and the other people who had donated bedding went back to the school and everything they had loaned was there. "We washed everything, put it on the line, and all was good," Sue remembers. "Some people said, 'Well, I don't want mine back. I'll throw it out because some stranger used it.' But I thought, 'Some poor stranger had to sleep on my bedding.'"

Ron volunteered at Gander Collegiate. They asked him to arrive at 4 a.m., since the first plane sending people their way wouldn't begin deplaning until the middle of the night. When he showed up, there were some other men there from the Lions Club. They asked him to help scrub the floors so everything would be clean when the plane people arrived. Later they asked him to help make breakfast. Ron's job was to make toast.

Sue was working at the Gander Credit Union that same day. She remembers how a come-from-away Irish couple came in for a currency exchange. They had saved up to take a large group of kids to Disney World. Their shelter was a Salvation Army camp about thirty minutes outside Gander. They told her that the kids weren't disappointed at all at being diverted to Newfoundland; in fact, they were having fun. The woman told Sue, "The kids saw a bear and they thought they really were visiting Disney World."

BACK AT THE COLLEGE of the North Atlantic, I was getting up as the sun rose, brightening the classroom. The rest of the passengers woke, but Evan kept on sleeping. His snores were so loud, I laughed. Thankfully, classes were canceled.

When he finally got up, we focused on procuring some supplies. After spending all day in our clothes on the plane, plus sleeping in them, we were desperate for a change of underwear and socks, at a minimum. We asked around and were told there was a Walmart about three miles away.

It was a beautiful day, so Evan and I decided to walk there. But we didn't make it more than twenty-five yards down the road when a car pulled up next to us and rolled down the window.

"Where do ya need to go?" the driver asked.

We explained we needed clothes from Walmart.

"Hop in!"

My mother taught me never to get into a car with a stranger, but this felt okay. We had a nice conversation with the driver and his wife. When they dropped us off, they refused money. It was my first experience as a hitchhiker, and I didn't even need to stick out my thumb. Thinking back to 2001, it seems that Gander had invented modern-day ridesharing.

Inside the Walmart were dozens of stranded passengers. When we arrived at the men's underwear aisle, several men, including some elderly ones, stared at the emptied-out shelves as if they couldn't believe that underwear was so important. The standard-issue white briefs were gone, except for odd sizes. All that remained were bikini briefs and boxer shorts. Evan and I quickly grabbed some boxers, a package of white T-shirts, and tube socks.

After we checked out, we started walking back to the college and once again a stranger stopped and asked where they could take us.

Every person we came across was kind, friendly, and sympathetic about what had happened to America. It made me wonder if someone on TV had encouraged this sort of behavior, telling locals to provide transportation to the plane people. But that never happened. It didn't have to. That is just how they roll in Newfoundland.

The College of the North Atlantic was a fantastic facility to be stranded in. Aside from having many classrooms that had been converted into sleeping rooms, the college also had working phones. These were made available so every passenger could call their families around the world as often as they'd like, at no charge, even though the long-distance bill to the college would total thousands of dollars. The college also had a computer lab people could use to send email to their loved ones and to read news.

Best of all, the college offered a commercial cooking program with a full kitchen. One evening the volunteers whipped up two hundred stuffed chicken breasts for dinner. It tasted better than any meal we had been served at any restaurant on our European vacation.

How did they suddenly find two hundred chicken breasts on such short notice in a tiny town? I couldn't help but be reminded of the Gospel story of "feeding the multitude," in which Jesus takes five loaves of bread and two fish and performs a miracle that feeds the five thousand people who have gathered for his sermon — and He still has leftovers.

Sixteen years later, I finally learned how this mini-miracle happened. Marine cooking instructor Elizabeth Moss told me, "When we got word passengers were coming on the afternoon of September 11th, head chef

Barry Steele, myself, and two of my kids went shopping at all three grocery stores in Gander to find enough chicken. We charged all costs to the college, without limit. We bought enough chicken, plus other meat for sandwiches, and soup." She added, "Our culinary students had just begun, so they hadn't been trained in the kitchen yet. Still, they were a big help to us as volunteers."

Food donations began pouring in so quickly from church parishioners and the general public that there was no room for keeping food cold. In response, Mayor Elliott declared the town's hockey rink "the world's largest walk-in refrigerator."

Meanwhile, at Gander Collegiate, two passengers were identified as world-famous chefs. One fellow was from India, where he was a top chef at a resort in the Azores. Another man was head chef from a group of hotels. Ron Walsh was there in the kitchen, trying to help them.

"Neither one of them would let us help," he said. "They just said, 'No, no, this is our treat this time.'" The chefs took over the small kitchen, telling the volunteers what food they needed, including spices. The volunteers brought back everything they needed in no time and produced an enviable menu of chili and macaroni and cheese.

It felt like every stove in the Gander area was on, cooking nonstop for the come from aways. They baked

Newfoundland dishes, moose stew, or cupcakes, but they all made the same thing: comfort food.

EVAN AND I were fortunate that we didn't have to sleep overnight on the parked airplane, like some of the other refugees did. Passengers like Nick Marson and Diane Kirschke.

Nick, from the United Kingdom, and Diane, from Houston, were both traveling alone on Continental Flight 05 when their plane was diverted to Gander. After they woke on the morning of September 12th, airport officials sent breakfast out to their plane. They spent over twenty-five hours in their aluminum tube before deplaning into the Gander airport.

Nick and Diane were separated from the rest of the Continental flight because they needed medications and they weren't allowed to access the checked luggage on their plane either. Diane went with a volunteer to the Salvation Army shelter in Gander and Nick went via a school bus directly to the Society of United Fishermen (SUF) hall in Gambo, a half-hour's drive away. The Salvation Army gave Diane soup and a sandwich, but then they realized the sleeping quarters were full to capacity, so she was taken by a volunteer to the SUF in Gambo.

The volunteers in Gambo went to the nearby military base to retrieve cots and blankets for more than eighty visitors. More than a dozen volunteers were there helping out at all times, with four men spending the night to help with whatever needs the passengers had. Nick and Diane met each other while waiting in line for their military-issue blankets.

Since she seemed friendly to him, he asked if he could camp next to her cot. She agreed. After hours of watching the images on TV, they had had enough. They joined a married couple on a walk down the gravel road to sightsee in Gambo. The other couple turned back because the woman was wearing heels and couldn't manage the rocky road. Nick and Diane continued on just the two of them, and after walking a while, they stopped at a small convenience store to buy a beverage. Nick was stunned when Diane paid for his drink.

"As a gentleman, I'd always been the one to pay," Nick would later tell me. "Who was this woman who did this?"

Nick liked Diane's assertiveness, so he ended up spending the rest of his time while in Gambo with her. After being so close over a few days, they both found they had feelings for each other. The spark of romance between two strangers was kindled in Newfoundland. Nick transferred to Texas, where they were married. They returned to Newfoundland for their honeymoon in September 2002, which coincided with the first anniversary of 9/11.

NEXT-DOOR AT THE HIGH SCHOOL, Ron Walsh got to meet people from everywhere. He really enjoyed speaking to the international passengers from a Lufthansa flight and a Continental Airlines flight. But he noticed that there was one Arab family — a husband, wife, and little girl — who seemed unnerved.

"Only the husband spoke a bit of English. They were by themselves, alone all of the time. I went over to introduce myself anyway. I made sure they were comfortable," Ron remembered. "They were the loneliest people there. The word was already coming out on the news that these attacks were probably linked to Osama bin Laden. I thought, 'That little girl has nothing.' So I went down to Walmart and I found this sweet little blue plush teddy bear. I went back to the school and told the father, 'I have this gift for your little girl.' He agreed it was okay to give it to her. The wife and I cried. Then every time they would come down to the cafeteria for a meal, they would come see me. They felt safe with me as their contact."

At Gander Academy, the town's elementary school, an Egyptian woman who lived in Gander arrived with vegetarian food because she assumed some of the passengers would be Muslims and knew they often wouldn't eat meat unless it came from a Muslim butcher. While at the school, she started to cry because she heard that one of the hijackers in the U.S. was Egyptian. She worried about discrimination and retaliation against Muslims.

Meanwhile, one of the Muslim passengers was so moved by the kindness of strangers that he asked the librarian where he could buy a plaque in Gander so he could present it as a thank-you. The librarian told him about a local marble shop and helped him with his English for the inscription. The man went out and paid to have the plaque done while he was still there. It read,

To the students and teachers of Gander Academy, thank you for sharing your school.

He called everyone together at the school to present it to the principal, on behalf of all the passengers. Gander Academy housed hundreds of stranded passengers from four different planes. The plaque still graces the wall of the library.

Newfoundlanders seemed to emanate empathy to all the plane people. They treated each person with respect and made accommodations for all kinds of people without thinking twice. As a gay couple, we were certainly treated with kindness like everyone else. It seemed like they were ready for any kind of challenge thrown their way, and maybe even thrived on problem-solving.

ON SEPTEMBER 12TH, I successfully placed a call back to my office in Austin. The staff had assembled in the conference room and I spoke with everyone via speakerphone. They helped me better understand the national magnitude of what had happened.

All U.S. airspace was still shut down and nobody, including the airlines, knew how long it would be closed. Businesses had shut their doors out of fear of additional terror attacks. It was serious. One person said, "I don't think you understand. There is no advertising running on any TV station and almost every cable TV station is showing nothing but news about the attacks."

The conference room at my office had been turned into a crisis "war room." Normal business had been shut down and this war room had one objective: to get me home. Each staff member was researching some way to do just that.

They had a world map on the wall with a big circle drawn around Newfoundland. Someone researched ferry service from Newfoundland to Maine. Because every rental car in the U.S. was taken, another staff member researched how to buy a car for me to pick up at the U.S.-Canada border. But the borders were closed. I was grateful to have such caring, resourceful people helping me remotely.

At lunch that day, I had a remarkable small-world connection. I turned to a nice woman sitting across from me and introduced myself.

"Where are you from?" I asked.

"New Jersey," she said.

"What do you do there?" I asked.

"I own a PR agency."

"Wow. I own a PR agency," I said. "Who are some of your clients?"

"One of our biggest clients is a company called Trex. They make outdoor decks from a composite of wood and recycled plastic," she said.

"I know Trex! We just bought a Trex deck for our backyard. My PR firm focuses on environmental issues. In fact, one of our clients is America Recycles Day. I remember talking to someone two years ago about a donation of Trex for a national contest. We built and gave away the American Green Dream Home," I said.

"Uh, that was *me* you spoke to!" she said.

Maureen Murray and I couldn't believe we had spoken by phone several times to arrange a publicity photo. Later, she remembered we had briefly met at a convention two years before and she'd taken a picture of me with her client. But there we were, stranded in Gander, sitting at a cafeteria table at the College of the North Atlantic. We had even more in common.

Maureen introduced me to her lesbian partner, Sue Riccardelli. I introduced them both to Evan. Maureen had somehow also met another single gay man from Houston on our plane. We could've formed our own support group of LGBT Americans stranded at the college.

At Gander Academy, someone delivered a giant box of men's underwear. Diane Davis went on the school's intercom to announce, "We just had a box of men's underwear delivered. If you want some underwear, please line up at the counselor's office. For all you Brits on Virgin 21, that's 'knickers'."

Although Diane was working nonstop at the school, she offered strangers access to her home across the street, so they could take a shower. She told two African women wearing traditional dresses to use the shower at her home.

"When they returned, they told me, 'We knocked and knocked and nobody answered.'" Diane had left the front door unlocked, but the women didn't understand that it was indeed Diane's house and that they did have permission to go inside and help themselves to the comforts of home. What was a practical consideration for a woman like Diane seemed unthinkable to the recipients of her radical generosity. Diane laughed as she explained, "I had to walk them across the street to assure them they could go inside."

Also at the academy, an elderly passenger was exasperated trying to reach his son, who worked in the World Trade Center. He needed help, so he went to the best resource expert around: the librarian. The man had a business card for his son, which showed his work address. The librarian interviewed him about all the facts, and she tried calling a number of agencies in New York City. They had no luck when they first tried to locate him. Two days later, the man finally remembered the name of his ex-daughter-in-law. The librarian found her name using directory assistance and called her. Thankfully, she said she had spoken with the man's son. Although the son had been in the World Trade Center at the time of the attacks, he had made it out safely.

# CHAPTER 4

---

## We Stink and We Want to Go Home

SEPTEMBER 13TH

THERE WERE NO showers at the college, so by day three we all began to stink. Evan and I met volunteer Terry Dechman, who worked at the college. She and another coworker volunteered to drive us to the military base athletic facility, which was offering passengers use of their showers. Afterward, they drove us around the airport to take a look. It looked like an airplane graveyard because it had so many planes but none of the noise or fumes of jet engines.

Standing outside the airport fence, within view of our quiet Air France plane, I recorded an interview with

Terry on my video camera. I asked her, "So, what's it like having all these visitors?"

She replied, "Actually, it's been kind of fun. I work at the College of the North Atlantic, and that day [9/11] we had an emergency meeting at 3 p.m., and we were told we would be bedding down some of the passengers. Everyone got into the spirit of things, I think. I got a call at 7:30 that night to go up to the college. We were told Air France passengers would arrive at 8 p.m., but they didn't get there until 10 p.m."

She paused for a moment before continuing to describe the incoming passengers.

"You could see they were absolutely stunned by what had happened. One of the things that was really helpful that we did was set up several TVs in the cafeteria. They didn't have any information. I was amazed by how absorbed they were in seeing what happened in America twelve hours before.

"I took a family home with me. I identified a family with a young child, about eighteen months. I myself have traveled with an infant, and I know how difficult it can be. They were from Burlington, Vermont. So I got to know one family quite well."

By late afternoon on Thursday, September 13th, signs were posted around the college announcing a last chance for passengers to meet with the crew. Up to that point, several of us had wondered where the airline crew was. Since leaving the plane we had received no updates from Air France. Everyone gathered in the school cafeteria. Captain Hollande spoke first in French and then in broken English. The head flight attendant spoke in German, and another flight attendant spoke in Italian.

"We are very touched by the kindness that we have received here. We are very touched by it," they said. The passengers applauded. One passenger created a donation box using an old cardboard box. A teenager wrote SCHOLARSHIP FUND on it, using black Magic Marker.

She and a friend passed the box around the cafeteria, just like you'd see during a collection in church. Evan and I dropped U.S. dollars in the box, while others added other currencies. We later learned thousands of dollars were donated that day. The college did create a scholarship, which they awarded to students who exemplified kindness to fellow students. Several donors continued to send money over the years, but the scholarship eventually ran out of funds after fifteen years. Everyone considered fifteen years a great run, considering the college never solicited a dime.

The captain continued. "Now for the future: We didn't meet you before now because we didn't have any serious information to give. Now we know we will leave tomorrow morning. We are supposed to leave. We hope to leave. I don't know at what time. It won't be early, so you can sleep as much as you want. You will be informed in time."

Then came a surprise. "There are two possibilities: The first is that we fly to New York. The second, we fly to Paris." When the captain said this, there were audible gasps of confusion.

He explained, or tried to explain—it was clear the facts were still coming in—that while they had thought they would simply continue to fly via Montreal to our intended final destination, that didn't look like it was going to be possible and the quickest way for us to get home would be to return to Paris and then board new flights to New York once U.S. airspace reopened.

"It doesn't make sense to fly all the way back to Paris!" someone said.

"That's burning a lot of gas!" an American man screamed.

An Italian man said in accented English, "That is unusual. That is unusual."

The German flight attendant tried to calm the crowd. The language barrier was making this all very confusing.

We didn't want to go back to anywhere in Europe at a time when war had broken out. What if the attacks started again when the airspace reopened? What if the U.S. decided to take weeks before allowing anyone to fly into the country? We wanted to wait it out in Gander until we knew we would get back on home soil.

Back at the college, Evan and I went to the computer lab to email my office about this latest news. If we went back to Paris, would we really be on our way back to

Austin in a few days? Or could this attack provoke a counterattack, which could leave us stuck in Paris? In some ways, being stranded in Paris didn't sound that bad—unless war broke out. What if we were stuck there for a month or longer? I had clients I needed to get back to.

The email reply came back: "Don't go back to Paris!"

I went to Mac Moss to inquire about other options for getting to the U.S. besides air travel.

"Well, there's a bus that goes once per day to the west coast of Newfoundland. That takes six hours," Mac began. "Then you could catch a ferry across the Atlantic Ocean to Nova Scotia. You should know the seas might be rough because there's a hurricane brewing down to the south. That ferry takes nine hours."

He paused for a second before continuing. "From there, you might be able to catch a bus to the train in Halifax. You can take the train from Halifax to the U.S. border at St. Croix, Maine, assuming the border is open by then. Then you'd have to drive to Austin, that is if you can find a rental car or a bus or train."

I did the math. Without including stops, it would take fifty-seven hours to get to Austin, Texas, and would take two and a half days just to get to the U.S. border. All of this would cost well over $3,000 for both of us.

Then came the false alarm. News came out that the airspace would be reopened, so we were given just a couple hours' notice to prepare to board school buses back to the airport. Flight crews got dressed and went to the airport, ready to go at a moment's notice. Then something happened.

As it turned out, U.S. airspace was not yet reopened. The news came that we were *not* leaving yet. They told us they would give us a four-hour notice. So we could relax, so long as we stayed close to our shelters in case new departure instructions came out.

American Airlines captain Beverley Bass had a telling experience during this "false alarm." She and her crew were dressed and ready to go at the Gander Airport when they heard the news about the additional delay. They would return to the Comfort Inn, which was now beginning to feel like home to them. There really isn't a significant taxi service in Gander, and no one was around to give them a ride.

Beverley's team was frustrated, standing curbside at the airport, just waiting. At that moment, Beverley looked around and noticed two elderly women approaching them. One of the women, sensing their anxiety, opened up her bag and pulled out an accordion. She began to play "God Bless America."

"There wasn't a dry eye in the crowd," she said. A foreigner serenading a group of Americans with a patriotic song was so moving in light of the crisis in America. I wonder if Americans would do the same for Canadians if they were stranded in the United States?

BACK AT THE COLLEGE of the North Atlantic, people decided to get outside and take advantage of the beautiful weather. A group of young people played a game of soccer. It was a pickup game that included the Costa Rican rafting team and some Americans and Europeans. Everyone was having fun and getting along.

Evan and I were sitting in a classroom on the second floor watching the game from the window when we met Ted, an older gentleman from our flight. He was an American who lived full-time in Paris. He had been traveling to New York City to put his apartment up for rent.

"Where is your apartment?" I asked him.

"Lower Manhattan," Ted replied.

We sat in silence for a moment before Ted explained that the apartment wasn't adjacent to the World Trade Center, but it was nearby.

"I wonder if it's been demolished in the attacks," he sighed.

About this time, Sue and Maureen dropped by. Sue asked, "Do you want to go on a walk with us and two other ladies to nearby Cobb's Pond? Just to kill time."

I went and grabbed Evan, and we nudged Ted to join us as well. I grabbed my video camera.

The other two women on the walk were Glennis Rasmussen and Liz Tanner, sisters-in-law from Minnesota. They were also returning home from a European vacation. We walked along the beautiful pond trail until we saw an area with benches, where we all sat and talked.

Evan entertained the group with our story about how this was the second time we'd been stuck without our suitcases on this trip. The first stop on our vacation had been Nice, France. We flew there via Paris and somehow our luggage didn't make the connection.

"They gave us a toothbrush, but after a day, we needed new clothes. So we went to a local grocery store called 'Monoprix,' where we each bought underwear, socks, and a cheap tourist T-shirt. We looked like we'd robbed a Goodwill box!" he said to roars of laughter.

Soon we were comparing stories about the amazing generosity we'd received in Gander. Sue said, "I came down for breakfast, and I was shocked that the volunteers at the college had made French toast and bacon. Someone rudely asked, 'Don't you have any scrambled eggs?' I couldn't believe it. I thought we'd be fortunate to have doughnuts and hot dogs. Maureen told the guy, 'These people are giving their all here, and you're asking for eggs? You're lucky we are not living on Cheez Doodles from the mini-mart.' This place has a culinary school. It's been constant food like you'd see on a cruise. I think we gained ten pounds."

Like others, Sue and Maureen witnessed Gander's on-demand transportation system. "We were walking up to the corner store when a car stopped," said Sue. "He offered us a ride and we said, 'No thanks.' Then a second car pulled up. Same thing. It happened three times!"

Ted chimed in with a similar story. "I was just taking a walk down the street when a car pulled over. I thought, 'Have I done something wrong?' The driver wanted to know if I needed a ride anywhere and I had to say, 'I'm just trying to take a walk around your lovely town!'" We all laughed.

The air was getting chilly, so we all agreed to return to the college. Soon after we arrived back, we got the word from Mac that buses were on the way to the college to take us to the airport. *Hallelujah*, I thought.

As we were leaving, the college staff provided a final moment of kindness. They had packed to-go bags of snacks and fruit. They guessed—correctly, it turned out—that our plane wouldn't be restocked with provisions for another flight. As we picked up our food, the volunteers lined the driveway to say goodbye.

I'll never forget one woman who cried, "Don't go!" I wasn't sure if this was because she was worried about our safety, or if she really enjoyed the companionship of 272 new friends.

# CHAPTER 5

---

## Déjà Vu — Back in France

SEPTEMBER 14TH

AFTER EVAN AND I arrived at the Gander airport, we checked in at the counter and confirmed that our destination was New York. The screening of carry-on bags seemed to take forever, as brand-new regulations meant you couldn't have any liquids or anything sharp like tweezers and razors.

At the security gate, the agent informed us that our plane was in fact flying back to Paris. President Bush decided to only reopen U.S. airspace to American airplanes, and Air France wanted their jet back. I quickly recalled what Mac had told me about ways to get back to America without taking a plane. I asked the gate agent, what would happen if I didn't want to go to Paris but wanted to take the bus and ferry. She said we could not do this now. We were required to stay inside the secured area.

Our airline captain tried to dissuade those who wanted to travel to America by land and sea, because a hurricane was coming and he understood there were only two ferries available to cross the ocean from Newfoundland to Nova Scotia. He said, "Newfoundland took care of you up to now, but if you walk out the door, you are on your own."

I didn't like either of my options. Inside the international departures lounge, I went again to the pay phone and made two collect calls. First, I called the office. Back in the Austin conference room, the staff took a vote. It was unanimous: Don't go back to Europe. Two staff members generously volunteered to drive thirty-six hours from Austin to the U.S.-Canadian border in Maine to pick us up and drive us home (if the border was open). This seemed safe, but it would be an agonizing journey for everyone.

My second call was to my parents, which Mom immediately answered. I told her the situation—that essentially we had been lied to by the airline about our next destination. "Don't get on the plane!" Mom cried.

I hung up, not sure what to do. I hated to disobey my mother's orders, but in my mind I was trying to project which course home would be the less stressful for both

Evan and me. It would be a strenuous journey by bus and ferry, but under the circumstances it didn't feel good to put more distance between ourselves and home.

My primary fear was being stuck in Europe for an extended period when I needed to get back to work at the office. I smiled. I could hear the voices of friends back home in my head, saying, "Oh, poor you, stranded in Paris!"

Fourteen of the other passengers refused to board the plane once they learned the flight was heading back to Paris. They were content with abandoning their luggage for good. A security guard at the airport helped them charter a bus for $1,500 apiece. The bus would pick them up at 7:30 the next morning to take them to the border. They made a return trip to the College of the North Atlantic for one more night.

Evan wanted me to make the decision.

I knew that if we stuck with the airline, they would be obligated to get us to our final destination, with our bags full of clothes and European trinkets intact. If we decided to try a different route, it would be exhausting for everyone, expensive, and we would never get our possessions again. So, we stayed with Air France.

At least another hour went by before we could board. By the time we left the terminal and walked out onto the tarmac, it was cold and dark. I could see our plane with its engines running. That was a good sign.

But instead of going to the plane, we were first directed to a school bus. Nobody told us why. After the bus was loaded, we drove across the runway with a police escort, lights flashing. I was mentally exhausted, hoping I had made the right choice. Evan turned the video camera on me and captured me with my head buried in my arm, resting on the seat in front of me.

The bus stopped at a giant airplane hangar. Inside were thousands of pieces of luggage. We were told to go to a certain area, identify our bags, and gather them so that they could be retagged and loaded onto our plane. It took another hour or more for everyone to identify their bags and board. It was stressful to be leaving the safety of our adopted home and once again be encountering decisions that involved factors so outside of my control. In only a matter of hours, I had gone from feeling incredibly relaxed, sitting beside Cobb's Pond talking to strangers about our gratitude for the many kindnesses we had received, to being upset and anxious, wondering if I had made the wrong decision.

Ultimately, we took off into the night, eastbound over the Atlantic Ocean, flying back to Europe.

WHEN WE LANDED, it was morning in Paris. We were told to enter the terminal and that we would receive a voucher for a hotel near the airport. No information was given about rebooking our flights.

"Come back to the airport in a couple of days," an Air France representative told everyone.

After receiving our voucher, we entered the main terminal. As we walked in, we saw that every single person was standing frozen and quiet. It took a while to realize that thousands of people in a foreign country were having a moment of silence for the victims of the attacks in our country. They played "The Star-Spangled Banner" on TV and over the airport's public address system.

It wasn't just the airport that stood still. People all across Europe's highway systems stopped their vehicles and got out to stand at attention for this peaceful show of love for America.

It was truly moving, and I'll never forget it. I wondered if we, as Americans, would ever make the same gesture for citizens of a foreign country. America helped other countries when they had crises; now it was our turn to deal with terrorism, and the rest of the world wanted to pay respect to America.

As soon as the moment ended, the airport erupted back into the chaos that is typical of airports. And this morning there were thousands of stranded passengers inside and outside the terminal. Surprisingly, we got our luggage without any problems. That's when we said goodbye to Sue and Maureen. They would try to get the next flight back to Newark.

They spent the night in a fleabag hotel Air France paid for, then returned to Charles de Gaulle Airport at

5 a.m. After much confusion they were given "refugee status" with bright orange tickets. They were put on a Continental Airlines flight that departed at 7:30 p.m. and landed in Newark at 11 p.m. They told me that they were incredibly anxious during this second journey across the Atlantic Ocean, and it seemed to take forever. Stepping into the terminal, Sue, Maureen, Liz, and Glennis got into a huddle, hugged each other, and then kissed the Newark Airport floor, even though it was dirty.

Evan and I wanted to stay completely away from the New York area, so we got put on a waiting list for a flight direct from Paris to Houston on Continental Airlines. It would just be an hour's flight from there to home in Austin.

We said goodbye to our new friend Ted. He wasn't returning to New York; he was going back home to his flat in Paris. He offered to let us come and stay with him, but we thought it would be easier to get back to the airport for a standby ticket if we stayed nearby.

As I walked out of the airport, I silently said the Lord's Prayer. Somehow we found a shuttle to the Hotel Ibis, which was near the airport. It was a two-star hotel, and that was being generous with the stars. We checked in midafternoon, and even though it was a tiny, dirty hotel room, Evan crawled straight into bed, feeling sick. At least they had a small cable TV with the English news from BBC playing live coverage from America. I wasn't going to stay holed up there watching the planes hit the buildings for the twentieth time.

The hotel had a working telephone, so I called Sara back at the office and asked her to do the phone tree update saying that Evan and I were safe, back in France, where we had started our journey home days ago. I decided to take the train to downtown Paris to wander around.

When I arrived downtown, it felt different than it had just one week before, on what I thought would be our last day in Europe. As usual, there were couples strolling arm in arm, and many bicycles and small cars driving on the narrow streets (none of which stopped to pick up this unintentional hitchhiker), but this time it was more subdued somehow. A digital sign on the Champs-Élysées read "Americans who need assistance should contact the U.S. Embassy."

I spotted Notre Dame Cathedral. I needed to pray.

As I crossed the street and headed in that direction, I began reciting in my head the "Peace Prayer," also known as the Prayer of Saint Francis, that begins, "Lord, make me an instrument of thy peace." Actually, I was singing the prayer in my head. At a concert for a civic choir in Austin, Evan and I had sung this prayer set to beautiful music. In church growing up, I had sung another, more popular version from 1967 titled "Make Me a Channel of Your Peace," written by Sebastian Temple.

Considering the hatred of this terrorist attack, the lyrics resonated deeply in my heart, especially "Make me a channel of your peace; Where there is hatred, let me bring your love ... where there is despair in life, let me bring hope." The song goes on: "It is in pardoning that we are pardoned; in giving to all people, we receive; And in dying that we're born to eternal life."

Some might say it was too soon to look for joy, much less forgiveness. My faith was telling me that even in this darkest hour, I should be a witness for good. I certainly saw good all about me in Gander.

I went to a packed afternoon Mass at Notre Dame Cathedral, all spoken in French. I don't speak French, but I knew enough to know they were praying for their friends in *les États-Unis* (the United States).

OVER THE NEXT twenty-four hours, we both stayed in bed, watching news coverage from America and eating from the awful hotel restaurant. Attempts to reach the airline by phone were futile. But on Sunday, September 17th, we made a plan. We didn't want to haul all our bags to the airport if we weren't going to get a ticket that day. So I took a few bags and headed over to the airport. I told Evan that if he didn't hear from me after a few hours, he should bring the rest of the luggage and come to the airport as well.

There were thousands of people waiting in enormous lines at every check-in counter. I moved a few inches each hour. I decided that I wasn't going to wait in a giant line only to be told to go home again. Most of the people in line had been on flights to America on September 12th, 13th, and 14th. Surely, I thought, our September 11th flight would have priority. The only problem was talking to someone from the airline. So I did the unthinkable.

I cut in line, in front of hundreds of people.

One woman busted me doing it. "Are you cutting in line?" she said.

"Look, I was on a flight that left here on September 11th, and we got diverted to this other country for days, and then they flew us back here!"

She nodded and let me move into line in front of her. This allowed me to merely get to the desk and confirm that we were on the enormous standby list.

Soon Evan showed up at the airport as planned. "Why didn't you call me?" he asked.

"I had no way to get out of this long line and find a pay phone," I said. "I still have no idea if we will get a ticket home for today."

When we finally talked to the reservations agent at the desk, I decided that we wouldn't deal with Air France anymore. Continental had rushed an extra plane to Paris to help with the backlog of stranded passengers, so we hoped we would get on their direct flight to Houston. We were sent to another enormous line, where we were told that the airline would be holding a lottery for standby tickets.

"A lottery? We've been trying to get home since the 11th!" Evan said.

There were hundreds of anxious people waiting in a noisy terminal, and the two employees at the desk conducting the lottery didn't have a PA system to broadcast the names of the winners. Even when they tried to speak up it was nearly impossible to make out their words amid the crowd. They called out the first name: "Smith, Ted Smith, party of four."

The ticket agents looked around but didn't see Mr. Smith, who was actually only fifty feet away. So they called another name, convinced Mr. Smith was a no-show.

"Wait!" Mr. Smith yelled, and he grabbed his bags, wife, and kids and squeezed his way past the other passengers to reach the counter.

He got his tickets, and the crowd cheered for him! The next name was called, and hardly anyone could hear the name. The crowd was getting angry. Did they call our name? People shouted, "Speak louder! We can't hear back here!"

Eventually the crowd devised its own communication system. Someone near the desk would hear the name called. This time it was "Sanchez, party of six." They would then turn around and yell, "Sanchez, party of six!" Twenty feet back, another person would hear

Kevin Tuerff

Immediately after the September 11th attacks, U.S. airspace is closed and my flight over the Atlantic Ocean is diverted to the Canadian island province of Newfoundland and Labrador.

That day 122 transatlantic flights divert on the East Coast and 38 of them land in Gander, making for a total of 6,595 passengers and crew stranded in a town with a population of 9,000 people.

From my window seat, I can see armed police officers stationed at each of the thirty-eight stranded planes.

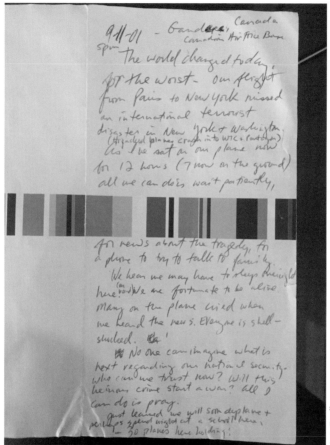

9-11-01 - Gander, Canada
Canadian Air Force Base
5pm
The world changed today,
for the worst - our flight
from Paris to New York missed
an international terrorist
disaster in New York & Washington
(Hijacked planes crash into WTC & Pentagon)
As I've sat on our plane now
for 12 hours (7 now on the ground)
all we can do is wait patiently,

for news about the tragedy, for
a phone to try to talk to family.
We hear we may have to stay the night
here. We are fortunate to be alive.
Many on the plane cried when
we heard the news. Everyone is shell-
shocked.
No one can imagine what is
next regarding our national security.
Who can we trust now? Will this
heinous crime start a war? All I
can do is pray.
Just learned we will soon deplane +
perhaps spend night at a school here.
~ 30 planes here holding!

Kevin Tuerff

After about seven hours of sitting in my seat, stranded on the tarmac in Gander, I start journaling on our in-flight menu.

Maureen Murray

Initially the volunteers struggle to locate enough bedding for their 274 unexpected overnight visitors from Air France Flight 004 at the College of the North Atlantic. After they put the call out, within hours, Gander residents donate enough sheets, sleeping bags, and pillows to turn the community college into a refugee shelter.

September 12th: Inside a classroom at the College of the North Atlantic, I'm happy to have a new, clean T-shirt and socks and underwear. Without our luggage, we had to go into town to purchase new clothes at Walmart. As we were trying to walk to the store, Ganderites graciously stopped to give us a free ride to any destination. Would we do the same in America?

After overdosing on TV news of the World Trade Center, many passengers decide to spend time outdoors on the lawn of the College of the North Atlantic campus in Gander.

PAY*IT*FORWARD
*9.11*

Inspired by the Pay It Forward Foundation, EnviroMedia staff would perform random acts of kindness on each anniversary of 9/11.

In teams of two, EnviroMedia staff members undertake their Pay It Forward 9/11 "kindness assignment:" to give away one hundred dollars to strangers. We often learned how the giver receives just as much or more than the recipient.

Kevin Tuerff

Mac Moss personally greets me at Gander International Airport in 2011, ten years after I was diverted there on 9/11.

Kevin Tuerff

Ten years later, gratitude in Gander: I join other come from aways to serve breakfast to volunteers like Nellie Moss and Sue Walsh.

Kevin Tuerff

Imagine if a stranger offered to give you a free flight in a small Cessna to get a close look at icebergs floating down from Greenland along Newfoundland's coast. I accepted this offer in 2011, and when invited to, I even took the controls to briefly fly the plane from the co-pilot's seat.

By kissing the cod I am screeched in as an honorary Newfoundlander.

The on-stage Kevin T. and the real-life Kevin T. Tony-nominated American theater actor Chad Kimball and me at a media event before a performance of the Tony-award-winning musical *Come From Away* on Broadway. The #gaylumberjack shirt, which Chad wears onstage eight times per week, is now a social media sensation.

The character Kevin T. sings the lead in "Prayer," a beautiful song that interweaves Christian, Jewish, Muslim, and Hindu prayers, and begins with the words "Make me a channel of your peace," from the Prayer of St. Francis.

In 2005, Austin reacts with Gander-like kindness when residents help New Orleans refugees forced from their homes by flooding after Hurricane Katrina.

Kevin Tuerff

During a 2016 trip to Gander, I meet members of the Alsayed Ali family, one of the first Syrian families sponsored and welcomed by Gander Refugee Outreach. Kindness to the stranger is clearly not a one-time thing for the people of Gander. They serve as a beacon to others, reminding us of the Golden Rule.

Carole Zoom

Me and my dear friend Alexis, who passed away in 2012. She and I attended the University of Texas at Austin together. I was at her hospital bedside when she died, too soon. Her last words were, "Don't be sad. All I want is good for the world. Love each other!" Alexis lived in Lower Manhattan during the attack on the World Trade Center. Five years after her death, I felt a calling to live in the same neighborhood.

The view of New York Harbor from my apartment in 2017. Only after I moved in did I realize this waterway was the last mile my grandfather would have sailed on his way to Ellis Island as an immigrant from Germany. I'm also just five blocks from the September 11 Memorial & Museum, formerly "Ground Zero."

Kevin Tuerff

I am joined by fellow Air France Flight 004 passengers Sue Riccardelli and Maureen Murray at the 2017 Tony Awards, where *Come From Away* was nominated for Best Musical.

Kevin Tuerff

The real characters who inspired *Come From Away* were surprised to watch a performance on Broadway with Canadian Prime Minister Justin Trudeau. I wanted to give him a copy of my memoir as a gift on the occasion of Canada's 150th anniversary of Confederation, but I was nervous about breaking protocol. I asked my new friends from Newfoundland if this would be appropriate and they enthusiastically said that I should do it. I thanked Trudeau for his leadership and compassion for refugees.

Canadians are especially proud of the story of Newfoundland's kindness to strangers on 9/11. Here I am speaking about my experience in Gander with musical-goers at the Royal Alexandra Theatre in Toronto. Mirvish Productions has seen record sales for *Come From Away* in 2017 and in 2018 is hosting a new all-Canadian cast.

it, and then turn around to the others behind him, and keep repeating the name until someone raised a hand and ran toward the front. It was like getting your name called on *The Price Is Right* game show. Come on down!

Names kept getting called, and none of them were ours. Evan and I were getting depressed; we just wanted to be home in Austin. I said another silent prayer that our names would be called. Finally, another airline employee came over. He had a louder voice. He yelled, "Tuerff, party of two!"

"*Here!*" I screamed. "I'm coming, we're here!"

I raced to the front and was handed two boarding passes. I later told my father it felt like I was getting called up for a ticket into heaven.

Security was tighter than ever, but when we finally boarded our plane and it took off, we breathed a little easier.

WHEN WE FINALLY made it home, I took two days off to recuperate. On my first day back at the office, I walked into the conference room and everyone was waiting for a surprise welcome-home celebration.

Every member of staff was wearing a red French beret, and many had penciled-in mustaches on their lips. They had beignets and champagne to celebrate and there was a giant "Welcome home" banner, which had been signed by the entire staff.

I was moved by what my colleagues had done for me, but by this time I had begun to see stories of compassion and kindness from all over the world. People had been holding candlelight prayer vigils on every continent. Thousands of first responders and average citizens drove cross-country to volunteer at the World Trade Center's "Ground Zero." Cabbies in New York City stopped honking their horns in traffic. The lineups of people waiting to donate blood to local blood banks stretched for blocks.

Tributes were held across the world. Even political enemies united in grief, hope, and solidarity.

After a few weeks, I wrote an email summary of our experience in Gander to share with my staff, family, and friends. The *Austin Business Journal* got hold of the email and a reporter wrote "An Exec's Newfound Grit." It was the first story about Gander's kindness to strangers. It appeared on September 30, 2001.

In November 2001, I got a call from Maureen in New Jersey that they had given my name to a producer at ABC News who had read a newspaper story about Gander. He was looking for video footage, and they remembered I had shot video while we were together. An hour later, I took a call from David Perozzi, a producer for ABC's *Primetime Live* show. He asked me about my experience in Gander and then asked me if I could send him the footage. He also asked if I would be willing to fly to New York for an in-studio interview for the show. At that time, many people were still afraid to fly, worried that more airplanes might be hijacked. I agreed to fly, and I brought Evan along for the trip to Manhattan so we could go see a Broadway show.

Sue Riccardelli had already been interviewed for the segment, but Maureen and Sue took the train into Manhattan to meet us for a fun reunion dinner. We all agreed that we'd been lucky to wind up together at the College of the North Atlantic under the leadership of Mac Moss, and again we recounted stories about how lucky we were, just as we had beside Cobb's Pond two months before.

We all found it was truly remarkable what everyone in this tiny town had done for us. We reflected on what it was that gave Ganderites their attitude of kindness to strangers. People told me that's just how they were raised. The people of Gander and all of Newfoundland have a deep sense of interconnectedness and compassion. They rely upon each other, especially during the harsh winter months. It's not uncommon for someone to spend hours snow-blowing a neighbor's driveway before their own. The cold temperatures keep them indoors a lot, so entertaining guests for meals, drinking, and dancing in their homes is a way to be happy.

I wished I could export some of that hospitality and kindness across the world. We've seen countless examples of people helping strangers after terrorist attacks and natural disasters, but why can't we treat each other this way on a regular basis?

WHEN IT WAS time for my interview with reporter Jay Schadler, a fancy Lincoln Town Car came to pick me up, and I insisted that Evan come with me. I had done plenty of TV interviews in my career, but I was nervous about coming up with a good sound-bite to accurately describe our powerful experience in Gander.

"You'll be fine," Evan assured me. "Maybe you could say, 'On that tragic day, the people of Gander restored my faith in humanity.'" I loved that, because it was authentic.

David Perozzi was very kind, giving us a personal tour of ABC News headquarters. Just one month prior, ABC had received a package of anthrax in the mail. That had started another U.S. terror scare involving offices around the East Coast. The anthrax killed five and put seventeen others in the hospital. Perozzi pointed out the "'thrax elevator" that had carried the mail. He tried to avoid riding that specific elevator, but he didn't seem afraid of working in the building.

The ABC story, called "Angels of Hope," aired in December 2001. We held a watching party for staff and friends at my office late that night. When they saw my face on the screen, everyone cheered. They used the video clip of the Eiffel Tower, with me narrating, "Here we are walking up to the Eiffel Tower on September 10th, I believe."

It felt odd to celebrate my national TV debut because it was related to 9/11, but I felt comforted knowing that

Americans could see and hear the story of light amid the darkness, via Newfoundland.

The reporter interviewed one of the Gander school bus drivers who'd broken the picket line to help with transportation. When asked why, the driver said, "We believe in doing good deeds for good people, especially the Americans."

Perhaps his sound-bite about good deeds would be my inspiration for what to do on the first anniversary of 9/11.

## CHAPTER 6

### Pay It Forward 9/11

WHEN WE LEFT Gander, the volunteers said our gratitude was enough and no repayment for the food or phone calls was necessary. Their generosity provided a beautiful example of how little things can make a big difference.

On the first anniversary of the attacks, in 2002, I wanted to go back to Gander, as some come from aways did. But the cost and time for me to travel from Austin to Gander would have been greater than a round-trip airfare to Paris.

I wanted to do something to offer my gratitude, but what? Sitting at my office desk, an idea hit me. I borrowed an idea from the popular book and movie *Pay It Forward* by Catherine Ryan Hyde. This touching fictional work demonstrates how a young boy could start a movement that promoted kindness to strangers. I wondered if there was a way to use that concept to demonstrate my gratitude for Gander. The U.S. was still anxious and angry about 9/11, but perhaps we could give people hope.

As a co-owner of a small business with forty employees, I decided to try encouraging my staff to spend a day doing good deeds for strangers. We would make it fun by breaking the staff into teams of two and giving each team a hundred-dollar bill. These teams could then use the hundred dollars for any act of kindness for strangers. Unsure whether staff would go along with this, I ran the idea by a couple of longtime employees. They wholeheartedly approved.

We closed the office on the morning of September 11, 2002, to allow time for the teams to do their work. Staff were instructed to perform random acts of kindness anonymously. But they were also told to try to explain the story of what had happened to their boss in Gander on 9/11. At the end of the day, we gathered in a conference room and each team explained how they had spent their money. People got teary-eyed as they talked about the amazing reactions they received when they did small things like buying someone a cup of coffee or giving away a bus pass to a stranger. There was something magical when they made that one-on-one connection, just as I had experienced when the teenager handed me his air mattress and pillows at the College of the North Atlantic.

Two teams ran into each other at the local charity hospital in Austin. Both had the same idea to visit the maternity ward to support a new mother who was giving birth to a baby that day. The nurses at the hospital told both teams that there were two single mothers who had given birth that day. Both mothers were certain to need the money. One team gave a card and a crisp hundred-dollar bill. The other team purchased a hundred-dollar savings bond and wrote a card stating: "Because your baby is born on a day that will always be linked to a day of tragedy, we'd like you to have something positive you may share with the child in future years."

Another team gave their hundred dollars to the owner of a breakfast diner, asking him to use the money to pay for the next several checks until the money ran out, probably after about eight tabs. He promised to remind customers that it was the anniversary of 9/11 and to encourage them to pay it forward by doing a good deed for a stranger that day.

Another team decided to break the hundred-dollar bill into a hundred singles. They paper-clipped a note to each one explaining Pay It Forward 9/11. They went to a busy street corner in Austin and tried to hand the dollars randomly to people in their cars at the stoplight. To their surprise, it was extremely difficult to get most people to roll down their windows to accept the gift. "What's the catch?" people kept asking over and over.

Being in the marketing business, we weren't surprised to find people skeptical of an offer of free money. Others gave an appreciative smile, or choked back tears, mentioning they'd known someone who died that day. One team spent their cash buying several tubs of ice cream and delivering them to local fire stations. Emergency first responders were always on someone's kindness list.

One year later, the word got out to the *Austin American-Statesman* newspaper, and reporter Andrea Ball hunted down someone who had received a gift the first year. She wrote: "One team gave $100 to the founder of Comfort House, which provides food, day care, and emotional support to children in a low-income neighborhood. 'Spend it on yourself,' they told her. She didn't. She spent it on the Comfort House food bank, buying enough supplies to feed fifty kids. She said, 'It did so much for us. I figured angels just gave me a gift.'"

Ball even tracked down Gander mayor Claude Elliott for the story. He said of the Gander 9/11 response, "We did the only thing we know how to do, which was to comfort them, console them, and show them some love."

That newspaper article blew my company's anonymous cover. I received an emotional voice mail message on my office phone that made that okay. The caller said, "Hello, Kevin, you don't know me. My name is

Vincent. I just wanted to thank you. This morning I had a flat tire. I took it to get fixed and one of your employees paid for it. At first, I was kind of puzzled about the whole thing, until just now at 3:00, I'm reading the front page of the newspaper. The article starts out, 'Something special could happen to you today.' And it did. I had no idea that any of this had occurred to anybody in Austin. But I want to thank you very much. It was very heartfelt. What you're doing is very kind, and you really made a difference in my life. I just wanted to thank you."

That difference cost exactly $7. Seven others with flat tires received the service for free that day. I got choked up listening to the voice mail. I thought, Maybe this is an example of what Matthew's Gospel in the Bible was encouraging— "Do unto others as you would have them do unto you."

I told Ball in the article, "Everybody's lives are so frantic and busy. Often it takes a jump start to remind us of the importance of being kind to strangers. It doesn't take a whole lot of effort to make an impact."

A WOMAN IN AUSTIN, not connected to the company, heard about the idea that morning and immediately decided to start baking. She and her husband had lived in the New York City area for many years, and some of their neighbors were killed in the World Trade Center.

She and her husband read about Pay It Forward 9/11 in the newspaper. After reading the article, they looked at each other, headed for the big chest freezer in the garage, grabbed the homemade cookie dough that could always be found there, and began placing it on baking trays. After hours of baking, they packaged the cookies into plastic sandwich bags, two cookies per bag, and tied each bag with a red, white, and blue ribbon, with a note saying, "Please do an act of kindness today in memory of those victims of 9/11."

Then the woman and her husband ran out the front door and began hopping on neighborhood school buses. They gave the cookies away, explaining that they were "free"... sort of. The only payment required was that the kids would promise to do an act of kindness. The bus drivers offered to take those cookies left over to the school offices for the staff. Everyone wanted to be included in what felt right and good to be doing.

This woman liked doing this so much that she called and left me a voice mail message. "Kevin, you don't know me but my name is Kitten, and I think this Pay It Forward idea to remember September 11th is fantastic."

She went on to describe what she did. A month later, I was in Washington, D.C., for work and I saw a college friend named John Howard, Jr., an appointee of President George W. Bush, at a conference. He said, "Hey, I heard about that Pay It Forward program. That was really cool."

I thanked him and told him about my voice message from the lady who made cookies. He asked, "Do you remember who she was?"

I said, "Sure, it was a funny name, like 'Kitten.'"

John started laughing hard, saying, "That's my mom! What a small world—right?"

Kitten and her husband, John Howard, Sr., would become two of the effort's greatest supporters, baking cookies for school kids every 9/11 for ten years. What they didn't expect was how many people in the Austin area had a connection to the attacks in Washington, D.C., and New York City. An office worker at one of the elementary schools said she counted on those cookies every anniversary of 9/11 because her brother had died in the towers and it hurt her so much that some young Americans didn't even know what 9/11 was.

"What we started in 2002 grew in joyful ways to our extended family, neighbors, several school districts, churches, and Girl and Boy Scouts," Kitten later told me. "Everyone wanted to be a part of the progress of America's coming together, day-by-day, week-by-week, and year-by-year. Everyone loved their role in helping the healing."

LIKE MANY PEOPLE, I was changed by 9/11. My experience in Gander motivated me to continue to grow the kindness initiative of Pay It Forward 9/11, but it also influenced my private spiritual life as well. My religious faith was rekindled. I started attending weekly Mass again. Even though I moved farther away, outside central Austin, I decided to stick with the University Catholic Center, my parish home that had helped me during my time of need in the early 1990s. I always felt welcome there. My prayer life was focused on peace.

In 2003, our company, which focused on doing good in the world, experienced a horrible betrayal that brought our company to its knees. It was a time filled with stress, anxiety, and paranoia. We needed an emergency infusion of cash to stay afloat. Sadly, our bank and many others wouldn't help us when we really needed money to bridge a cash flow gap. Thanks to my family, we secured a loan and then paid it off in less than a year. That September, when it was time for the second anniversary of 9/11, we had every reason to stop continuing our tradition. Instead, our hardworking staff pulled the company through the crisis. They really loved the Pay It Forward 9/11 initiative, so we kept it alive. We could've continued without the charitable expense of a hundred dollars per team, but it felt right to go on just as we always had, with the hundred-dollar bills.

Where there was despair, we kept hope.

By 2006, friends, family, and several businesses from Texas and other states had joined in our initiative. A local law firm joined in. Two of their employees distributed two hundred dollars by purchasing gas for strangers. They waited at the pump and surprised the drivers as they prepared to pay. Also that year, one EnviroMedia team gave twenty-five-dollar gift cards to four shoppers at a grocery store in a low-income neighborhood. Others handed out water and Gatorade to construction workers at a downtown site. Everyone felt they made a connection with other people in a way they had never before experienced. The staff considered this day the highlight of their year working at the company.

The Pay It Forward 9/11 initiative is included in the September 11th Families' Association's Seeds of Service exhibit at the new 9/11 Tribute Museum in New York City. The beauty of a grassroots movement like Pay It Forward 9/11 is that it takes on a life of its own. I was soon to find out that kindness spreads like wildfire and the heart of the Gander story was about to catch flame, this time set to music.

# CHAPTER 7

---

## The Return to Gander

BY THE TENTH anniversary of 9/11, people were starting to treat September 11th as just another day of the year. Since "Never forget" was the mantra of our country after the attacks, the leadership at my company decided to use our marketing skills to renew the idea of remembering the tragic day by doing even more good deeds or community service on its anniversary.

We donated cash and pro bono services to the California-based Pay It Forward Foundation to support their great philosophy, which had been inspiring our good deeds for the past ten years. I was able to talk by phone with the book's author, Catherine Ryan Hyde. She appreciated what we were doing and posted a YouTube video personally encouraging her foundation's supporters to join the tenth-anniversary effort.

EnviroMedia had grown in staff size to support thirty teams of two for the Pay It Forward 9/11 initiative in Austin as well as in Portland, Oregon, and Seattle, Washington. I would be bringing to Gander a $1,000 charitable donation to the College of the North Atlantic to contribute to the Air France Flight 004 Passenger Scholarship.

Throughout this time, I had been corresponding with friends in Gander. After ten years of giving thanks to Gander through my initiative, it was time for me to return to finally say thanks in person. Evan and I had unfortunately ended our relationship, so he wouldn't be making the reunion trip with me. Instead, I was joined by Melanie Fish, a friend and manager who worked at my company.

Melanie co-ordinated several requests from international news media, along with one from husband-and-wife writing team David Hein and Irene Sankoff, who told us they were working on a musical about Gander's role in 9/11. I thought this was a little odd, but I agreed to chat with them.

These days, it's still not easy to fly to Gander, even from New York airports. We started our journey to Newfoundland with a visit to the National September 11 Memorial & Museum in New York City. The names of those who died in the terrorist attacks are inscribed in bronze around the twin memorial pools. Melanie and I both felt the deep sadness of the tragedy. We didn't speak much as we walked around the memorial at what at the time was still commonly referred to as "Ground Zero." Before leaving, I made a donation for a cobblestone at the memorial plaza in honor of the people of Gander, Newfoundland.

The next day, we flew on Air Canada from Newark to Halifax to catch a connecting flight to Gander on a small regional jet. Alas, we were met with delays due to bad weather at Newark airport. We sat on the tarmac for hours before we took off. Later, when we landed at our connection, we could see the plane for Gander at another gate, so we hoped we wouldn't miss the connecting flight. We rushed to Canadian customs, but it took too long, and our flight left without us.

I was stranded in Canada once again. By this time it was 1 a.m., and the next flight to Gander would be another connecting flight through St. John's, Newfoundland, at 6 a.m. The next nonstop to Gander was much later in the day. The Halifax airport was deserted. Rather than sleep in the airport, we found a nearby hotel with two rooms available, deciding that four hours of sleep in a bed would be better.

Everything happens for a reason. If we hadn't missed that connecting direct flight, we wouldn't have met a special man on the connecting flight from St. John's to Gander. It was a small twelve-seater jet, much smaller than the 747 I flew on in 2001. When I started snapping photos out the window, a gentleman in front of me turned around and asked us where we were from. I explained that I was returning for the first time for a 9/11 passenger reunion. Melanie described what our company had been doing with Pay It Forward each year. Apparently, that moved him to do his own good deed.

"Would ya like to take a flight around the Gander area while you're in town?" he said with his thick Newfie accent. "Ya see, I own this plane, and I also own the flight school in Gander. We just got a brand-new four-seater Cessna. If you'd like, I'll have one of my pilots take you up for a spin on Sunday."

Of course we accepted this gracious offer. I asked if we might get to see the icebergs floating south from Greenland. I had read so much about climate change as part of my work and was looking forward to catching a glimpse of an iceberg in the wild.

When we landed at the Gander airport, the other passengers deplaned and we stayed behind for a few minutes. Melanie turned on our video camera and recorded me giving a few thoughts about being back in Gander since the chaos ten years prior.

"Almost ten years to the day, I'm back in Gander, Newfoundland. I was stranded here on 9/11 when our plane was diverted here. I'm on a much smaller, tiny plane right now. Back then, I was on the second of thirty-eight aircraft that were brought here to this small, tiny town. I'm excited to be back and see some of the folks to reunite from 9/11."

When I finally walked inside the terminal, there was Mac Moss, my 9/11 hero. The place looked a lot different from the time Evan and I had rolled in, tired after our long nightmare on Air France. In 2001, there were hundreds of volunteers there with tables of free food. This time, there were just a dozen workers doing their jobs.

A reporter from CBC Television (Canada's national network) was there to catch our airport reunion. He interviewed me and had me recount my memories about the place. Throughout the reunion weekend, I did several interviews with local, national, and international TV and radio reporters, and I did a live call-in interview at a local radio station. In true Gander fashion, Mac invited a newspaper reporter and photographer from Toronto back to his home for a cookout, which was photographed for the national newspaper, *The Globe and Mail.*

After years of telling this story, it never gets old for me. And still, I find that so many people have no idea about the generosity that Gander showed us that day. Humans need good role models, and the folks in Gander are truly that. I felt blessed to be a come from away, and motivated more than ever to spread the good news of hope for humanity even in our darkest hours.

Once we checked into our hotel, I was ecstatic to see Maureen and Sue there in the lobby. We had corresponded often, but this was the first time I'd seen them since 2001. Turns out they'd been visiting Gander on their summer vacation every other year.

Sue, Maureen, and I joined Mac and others for a special assembly with all the students of the College of the North Atlantic – Gander Campus. It was my first time back at the college, and it was strange to see students everywhere instead of haggard airline passengers, cupcakes, and sleeping bags.

The next morning, the Lions Club held a community breakfast at the hockey rink (a place Mayor Elliott had called the "world's largest walk-in refrigerator"). All the plane people who had returned for the reunion were invited to be servers on the buffet line. It was rewarding to be able to dish out scrambled eggs to people who had volunteered for Americans and other foreigners ten years ago. It was a way to finally show my thanks face to face. These people had inspired me to express my gratitude in so many ways over the last decade, but this—this was in person.

The commemorative events in Gander that I was a part of exceeded what most American cities (especially small towns) were doing to mark the 9/11 tenth anniversary. Perhaps Americans still didn't see anything good to celebrate. For America, the anniversary is a day of mourning. In Gander, it is a reminder of how they helped the world.

The musical writers, David and Irene, were in Gander for the tenth anniversary celebrations, too, and they were enjoying the local hospitality just as I had. The people they were interviewing invited them to stay at their homes instead of allowing them to rent a hotel room. Another person gave them the keys to his truck so they would have wheels during their stay—no questions asked. They interviewed the people who had volunteered as well as some of the "9/11 refugees," as the media had begun to refer to us.

I met David and Irene at the College of the North Atlantic one afternoon, and I told them about my experiences ten years earlier. I liked them right away.

Over the next several months we emailed and spoke by Skype. They also asked if I could send them my personal video footage from my days in Gander in 2001. I happily blocked off time on my busy calendar to talk with them. I did this because I hoped their musical could help the world learn about what happened in Newfoundland on 9/11, not because I ever imagined they would make me and Evan the inspirations for two characters in the show. Heck, there were more than 6,000 passengers that day, each of whom had a unique story.

They ended up making my story one of the central ones in the musical. I was flattered, but I also didn't know what kind of attention it would bring over the years to come.

There are a few fictionalized details that help make the show better, and don't bother me. In the musical, all the passengers are flying on Captain Bass's American Airlines flight. At Gander airport, just prior to their departure, she tells the passengers, "You booked a ticket from Paris to Dallas. I will try to get you to Dallas, but we may have to fly back to Paris." That never happened for her plane because American planes were allowed into the United States first. After that announcement, the ensuing chaos onstage is a wink to what happened to us back at the college when our Air France pilot made that very announcement. I had captured that particular uproar on video, with an Italian passenger yelling at the flight crew about how this flight plan was "unusual." David and Irene shared publicly that they'd rented a cabin in Ontario so they could focus on piecing together the story by digging through hundreds of hours of interviews.

One storyline in the musical highlights how Nick and Diane Marson met, fell in love over those few days, and ultimately got married. The writers also knew that Evan and I had broken up, and we weren't communicating. The scene was set: there was one couple who fell in love, and another who fell out of love. The timing of our break-up wasn't related to our experience in Gander, but I didn't mind because it helps tell the story.

In the musical, the gay couple tells others they live in Los Angeles, not Austin. Apparently one of the producers was concerned there were "too many Texans," with Captain Bass living in the Dallas–Fort Worth area and Nick and Diane living near Houston. I am often asked what it's like living in LA. I always chuckle, "I have no idea."

Another point of drama that was fictionalized for the show is that Evan and I never went to the Legion to get a drink. Why would we? We had two bottles of Grey Goose we were drinking at the college! We would get cups of ice and mixers, and secretly mix our cocktails in the men's bathroom, just in case drinking liquor in our shelter was forbidden. Therefore, I never did get to kiss the cod in 2001.

THE REUNION WITH the plane people was a cause for celebration, including a benefit concert at the hockey rink with The Navigators, a Newfoundland rock band. After arriving at the concert, Mayor Elliott asked me to speak to the packed crowd about my experiences in Gander ten years prior. Other speakers included representatives of Lufthansa Airlines, who donated a big check to the mayor. I wasn't nervous at all. I felt at home. I knew I was safe with the loving people of Gander.

"Hello, Gander!" I said, and the crowd cheered. "I was a passenger on the second plane that landed here ten years ago, and I experienced the amazing generosity of your kindness then. As one of many Americans who were here, I say thank you for giving me food, clothing, and shelter. I was at the College of the North Atlantic, and everyone we met there was fantastic! So thank you to everyone who volunteered."

I went on, "Every year on the anniversary of 9/11 at my company in Austin, we tell the story of Gander. We send out teams of our staff into the community and I give my employees a hundred dollars to use for doing good deeds for strangers and telling them about what happened here on 9/11."

I looked to Mayor Elliott. This was my first time to meet the mayor face to face, but still I challenged him to join me with confidence. "So, Mr. Mayor, I don't have a check for you, but I have a request. I want you in Gander to help me spread ten thousand good deeds across the world. We can prove that through darkness there is light, starting here in Canada. We can prove that we can all make a difference, one good deed at a time."

He smiled, the crowd applauded, and the next thing I knew, I was out dancing a jig on the dance floor by myself... and then several local ladies came up to dance with me. It was a blast.

ON THE MORNING of Sunday, September 11th, 2011, Melanie and I set out for that flight in a brand-new Cessna twin-engine airplane. This airplane was so new it had "new car smell" from the upholstered leather seats. We met our young pilot at the flight school. Melanie allowed me to sit in the copilot seat (I secretly wanted to learn how to fly a plane) while she sat behind me. The plane had high-tech navigation devices that made flying as simple as using a joystick. We put our headphones on and taxied the empty Jetway to the runway at YQX. No jumbo jets today—just us, cleared for takeoff.

The pilot had been told to take us for a spin around Gander. When I asked if we could see the icebergs, which were up near Fogo Island, about an hour-long round-trip, he said sure. We flew over the beautiful forests that cover most of Newfoundland until we reached the blue waters of the North Atlantic. Our pilot pointed out several chunks of icebergs. I asked if he could go low enough for me to snap some photos, which he did.

Mac Moss, who sails the ocean frequently, told us it's not uncommon to see floating icebergs but that seeing such big ones float south that late in the year definitely was uncommon. It was evidence of climate change that I'd only read about in research papers and news reports.

After seeing the icebergs, we set a course to return to YQX (Gander).

After a while, the pilot talked on his headset to Melanie and me. "Would you like to fly?" he asked.

Melanie almost passed out because she knew I would say yes. The pilot explained the basics of how to hold the steering wheel, flipped a few switches, and that was it: I was flying! It was exhilarating. I remember having dreams of flying like a bird on many nights back in 1997, when I started my company. This was just like in my dream. The pilot told me I should follow the navigation arrows on the computer screen and not just turn the steering wheel willy-nilly. The slightest movement in your hands would turn the aircraft off course.

All in all, I didn't fly for that many minutes, but it was one of the coolest things I've ever done. The pilot landed us safely back in Gander about fifteen minutes later.

Funny thing about the pilot: One week later, when Melanie and I were reviewing pictures of the Gander benefit concert, I noticed a familiar guy dancing behind me in one photo while I was on the dance floor. I emailed our pilot a copy of the photo. "Thanks again for the wonderful airplane ride over Newfoundland. By chance are you the guy dancing behind me in this photo?" I wrote.

"Guilty as charged," he replied.

MAC AND NELLIE invited me, Melanie, Sue, and Maureen to their house on Little Cobb's Pond for supper with their neighbors. It's a quiet, lovely place with beautiful trees lining the water, several minutes' walk from where we had sat together on our final day in Gander, back in 2001.

After supper, we were surprised to hear a giant ruckus in the house. Maureen, Sue, and Mac came around the corner wearing bright yellow raincoats and sou'westers (hats). One was banging on an "ugly stick," a traditional Newfoundland musical instrument made out of a mop handle with bottle caps and small bells. They informed us we were about to be named honorary Newfoundlanders, in a process called "the screech-in."

After eating some salty dried fish, Melanie and I were given a shot of screech (rum) as part of the ceremony.

"Is ye a screecher?" Mac asked.

Sue and Maureen had been screeched in years before. They told us how to respond: "'Deed I is, me ol' cock! And long may yer big jib draw!" It's a tongue twister. Translated, it means "Yes, I am, my old friend, and may your sails always catch wind."

After drinking the shot and eating a piece of Newfoundland steak (bologna), Mac anointed us by placing the oar of a rowing paddle upon each shoulder. Then it was time to kiss the fish, a Newfoundland cod. Lucky for us, the fish was frozen. We both kissed the fish, making it official. We even received a certificate announcing our honorary citizenship.

# CHAPTER 8

---

## Twelve Actors, Twelve Chairs, and Two Tables

THE HOUSE LIGHTS went down and the drums began. It was 2013, and I was in Toronto, Canada, sitting in the audience for the first version of the musical *Come From Away*, performed at Sheridan College.

After the first few minutes, my friend Michael leaned over and whispered, "Oh this is so good it'll go to Broadway."

I replied, "You don't know anything about Broadway. Only Disney musicals go to Broadway."

Little did I know what lay ahead. I assumed it would end with that college production. Instead, it was a snowball that gathered speed and support along the way in San Diego; Seattle; Washington, D.C; Gander; and Toronto.

A younger, better-looking, and immensely talented Tony-nominated actor-singer named Chad Kimball plays me. When asked how he felt when the person he portrays, his doppelgänger, was in the audience, he said: "If we were to do an imitation it would come off differently. Our director, Chris Ashley, gave us carte blanche to create the characters under the auspices of the true story. So I knew all about Kevin before we met, but I was able to create Kevin T. anew."

Chad and I have become friends and he is supportive of my efforts. He's not bothered playing a gay character even though he is straight. I shared with him how times have changed in entertainment's portrayal of LGBT characters.

As I sat there in the darkened theatre, I was absolutely rapt. And then Kevin T. — my character — began singing the song "Prayer." I couldn't breathe. It was like someone had sucker punched me. *How could they know?*

"Prayer" is based in part on the Christian hymn "Make Me a Channel of Your Peace." I'd always loved that hymn. It had played in my head for days after 9/11, and was sometimes the only consolation when I would see the continuous loop of TV footage of planes crashing into the World Trade Center. Its lyrics were on my heart when I attended Mass at Notre Dame in Paris on September 16th, 2001.

As a member of Generation X, I grew up primarily in a time of peace, when Americans were not engaged in war with another country. This hymn is based on the Prayer of Saint Francis, which extols the simple virtues of peace, love, and kindness to all.

> *Make me a channel of your peace. Where there's despair in life, let me bring hope.*

But how could my doppelgänger be singing this onstage if I never told anyone that this hymn had run through my mind? I didn't remember ever having told David and Irene about it.

The song develops into a beautiful harmony as Kevin T.'s singing is joined by the voices of other characters who add Jewish, Muslim, and Hindu prayers about peace in song. It is a very powerful three and a half minutes.

Michael Rubinoff, who first commissioned *Come From Away* for the Canadian Music Theatre Project at Sheridan College, shared an email with me from his friend Paul Akins, who had seen the full production. Paul wrote:

> I was bolted back into my Catholic childhood when "Make Me a Channel of Your Peace" began. It's a song that helped shape who I am today, but it also made me run for the hills when the Catholic Church made me feel shameful when I was a young gay man. The song tonight made me look at life differently. It allowed me to forgive, accept, and move on. What a

brilliant piece of theater—especially that very moving scene!

Wow. Through the beauty of storytelling, fifteen years after a hymn went through my head, I was able to connect with a stranger just like me, a gay Catholic struggling to remain faithful to an unwelcoming church.

When I came out of the closet at twenty-two, I was blessed by finding my support group of other gay Catholics in Austin, Texas, even though it ended in dissolution and disappointment. It was very difficult when the Bishop of Austin urged the Church leadership to stop the support group, but just having been in that group at all helped me realize that my identity and my faith could be consistent with each other.

Almost all my LGBT friends have left the Church due to hate speech from the Vatican and other Church leaders. I jokingly told others that I was "the last gay Catholic with my foot in the door." I hoped for change eventually, and I tried to influence hearts and minds by being visible while providing leadership, service, and financial support to my church.

I'm happy Pope Francis has now begun to heal the wounds of the past with welcoming comments, such as "If a person is gay and seeks out the Lord and is willing, who am I to judge that person?" Even better, Pope Francis has said that gays and lesbians are owed an apology by the Church, which has offended them.

I know that on a personal level, I felt a sense of belonging and acceptance in my support group in Austin, and I felt peace and kindness in Gander when they encountered me as a stranger in 2001.

IN 2014, THE SHOE was on the other foot. My 9/11 heroes Mac and Nellie Moss emailed to say they were visiting Florida soon, and they wanted to swing by Texas to visit me. This was their first trip to the Lone Star State.

These Gander folks set the bar of hospitality so high that I was anxious. First up, I greeted them at the airport with a "Welcome to Texas" sign. I also presented them each with a T-shirt that said "Keep Austin Weird" (the city's slogan). We posed for a photo near baggage claim after they landed. Because I lived in a one-bedroom apartment, I encouraged them to stay in a nearby hotel, but I made them a care package with some snacks, bottled water, "Don't mess with Texas" shot glasses, and some Texas tequila. They loved it.

After they checked in, I took them out to dinner and gave them a brief driving tour of downtown Austin. We visited the eclectic shops of South Congress Avenue, a Western wear store, and the Lady Bird Johnson Wildflower Center. The multiyear drought was letting up, and recent rains had delivered some beautiful flowers. We also visited Lake Travis and the famous

Oasis restaurant with its terrific view of the lake and the Hill Country.

I brought the Mosses by EnviroMedia to meet some of the staff who participated in our annual kindness initiative. I organized a special staff meeting so they could meet Mac and Nellie. Many of them knew the story of Gander through their annual participation in Pay It Forward 9/11, but I wanted them to hear it again, from the Ganderite perspective. It was a casual conversation, with staff asking several questions about the town's response. Mac and Nellie were generous with their compliments on the work the company was doing to protect the environment, and they were thankful for our efforts with Pay It Forward 9/11 in the name of Gander. That conversation was Nellie's favorite part of the visit.

IN THE SUMMER of 2016, after nearly twenty years of starting and managing EnviroMedia as president, my business partner purchased my shares and I stepped down from the company. At age fifty, I was starting a new chapter in my life.

When September came around, I wanted to carry on the Pay It Forward 9/11 tradition, but I had no staff to organize. I approached the producers of *Come From Away*, Sue Frost, Randy Adams, and Marlene and Kenny Alhadeff at Junkyard Dog Productions. They already knew the history of my annual tradition because it's mentioned in the show's script. I asked if the cast, band, and crew would like to join me on the fifteenth anniversary and everyone quickly agreed.

We gathered everyone in the Lincoln boardroom at Ford's Theatre in Washington, D.C., where the show was in production, to explain how each team had $100 to do at least three good deeds. Kenny Alhadeff made a passionate speech about the power of kindness and handed out the hundred-dollar bills to participants.

I saw the show for a second time that week, including a matinee on the afternoon of September 11. I had the honor of delivering a post-show discussion that afternoon and most of the audience stayed after the final curtain. The theater said it was the best attended post-show discussion ever. I explained the history of Pay It Forward 9/11 and how the cast and crew had participated that year. A few cast members told their stories of how they'd spent their $100 on random acts of kindness. Rodney Hicks, who plays "Bob" and other characters, explained his own surprise after jumping in line to purchase someone's lunch at a fast food restaurant. "I didn't realize how we don't look at each other in the eyes like we used to." He said, "Perhaps that's because we're all so busy with our heads down, buried in the electronic devices that are meant to connect us together."

After the show, several of my friends and I went to a nearby Greek restaurant for dinner. To everyone's shock, when the bill arrived, the waiter told us it was paid for by someone unknown! Inside our bill holder was a piece of paper that read "Pay It Forward 9/11." Everyone thought I was the person who picked up the tab, but I wasn't. I'd been organizing and promoting random acts of kindness for this effort for years, but this was the first time I'd been a recipient. We tried to guess who the benefactor was, but it's still a mystery.

My new freedom from a demanding day job allowed me to spend more time participating in these sorts of events related to *Come From Away*.

Before the show opened at Ford's Theatre in Washington, D.C., a city which suffered 184 deaths of workers at the Pentagon and the souls flying on American Airlines Flight 77 fifteen years prior, the producers had arranged a special performance for survivors and their family members. Kathy Dillaber, a retired Department of Army civilian and long-time docent for the Pentagon 9/11 memorial, attended the show. Kathy is a survivor, but she lost her younger sister, Patty Dillaber Mickey, who worked in a nearby corridor of the Pentagon, just fifty yards away. Kathy lost twenty-four workers in her office alone.

She was so moved by the story of Gander, she invited me and others whose stories are portrayed in *Come From Away* to visit the Pentagon and the 9/11 Pentagon Memorial. Lisa, a representative from the United States Department of Defense, arranged for our tour and escort into the Pentagon. We happened to arrive at the same time as an interior 9/11 remembrance, a closed ceremony for the Pentagon employees and their invited guests. We told Lisa that we would be honored if we could attend the ceremony, so she took us out to center court. It was a moving tribute from top military officials, with the playing of patriotic songs, including "Taps," by a Marine musician.

Afterward, Kathy gave me, Beverley Bass, and Nick and Diane Marson a special behind-the-scenes tour of the Pentagon so we could better understand what happened on the 9/11 attack. We visited the 9/11 memorial room and chapel and went to the outdoor 9/11 Pentagon Memorial, located on the side of the building where the attack took place. It is a moving memorial park with 184 benches, one for each victim: 125 Pentagon workers and 59 passengers and flight crew on American Airline 77.

In 2016, I was interviewed for a story about *Come From Away* for National Public Radio. Reporter Wade Goodwyn briefly explained my gratefulness and skepticism in the broadcast. He said, "As he flew away from Gander, Tuerff vowed to himself he was going to try to live his life like the honorary Ganderite he'd become."

Then came my voice: "They don't think that they did anything special and that we would do this for anybody at any time. But I wondered, would we — in America, would we do what they did? And I wasn't sure."

# CHAPTER 9

## Kindness and Refugees

REMARKABLE THINGS HAPPEN to me when I fly: I was diverted into the loving arms of Gander on 9/11. In 2011, on my return to Gander via St. John's, I met a stranger who offered to let me take a free, private aerial tour over Newfoundland in one of his personal planes, which I even got to fly myself. Then I had a spiritual encounter in the sky.

It was midday on September 12th, 2016, the day after the special performance of *Come From Away*. Shortly after my plane departed Ronald Reagan Washington National Airport, I was suddenly overwhelmed with emotion. It felt like I was intoxicated, but I promise I wasn't drinking Grey Goose vodka (or any alcohol). Thinking about the song "Prayer" from the musical, with its beautiful lyrics, which were so uncannily significant to me personally, I pulled out my iPhone to listen to some music. I wanted to hear "Make Me a Channel of Your Peace." I did a search for the word "peace" in my iTunes library and it turned out I had a couple versions of the Prayer of Saint Francis, along with other peace-related songs sung by Jackson Browne and Joan Armatrading.

As the music played, I was brought to tears. I opened my laptop to journal and began to type without thinking: "I am embracing my role as a channel of peace."

I felt a sense of joy, excitement, and bewilderment. It felt like God had taken over my fingers typing on the keyboard.

I spent days afterward wondering what my in-flight experience really meant. Two weeks later, I received an email from my dear friend who is a practicing shaman in New Mexico. We'd been friends since college in the late 1980s. His email asked, "Who is that friend of yours who died when we were in our twenties?"

I was unsure why he was asking, but I replied that I sadly remembered about a dozen friends who'd died of AIDS during my twenties. I listed their names: Bill, Javier, David, Tom, Gary, and the others.

My friend replied: "I sense Gary's spirit is with you and he's aware of what is going on in your life. Talk (pray) to him."

*Okay, that's freaky,* I thought. Yet the more I thought about Gary, the more vividly I remembered how it was he who gave me the courage to leave my comfortable state government job to start EnviroMedia. You see, in 1996, Gary had recently left his salaried job for a 100 percent commission-based real estate sales job. I was debating about starting a company without any investors, and I was nervous. Gary and I met at Texas French Bread in South Austin for lunch one day. I asked him, "Gary, what are you going to do if you don't make sales and end up without a paycheck?"

He assured me he was confident he would make money. He then asked me, "Kevin, when have you ever worked your absolute hardest and failed?"

I thought for a moment. "I can't think of a single time."

Gary said, "Then start that company!"

A few months later, I left my job and, with my friend Valerie, started the company that would occupy most of my time for more than nineteen years. It was wonderful to know that Gary was now here with me in spirit, at a time when I was beginning my next life chapter after leaving EnviroMedia.

A few weeks later, I was visiting my parents in Nashville. A friend of mine from college had lived there for many years. We kept up with each other via Facebook, and four years prior we had both suffered the loss of our mutual friend Alexis due to pancreatic cancer at age fifty-four. My friend invited me to dinner so we could catch up. I learned that she was studying to become a Buddhist chaplain. Shortly after we sat down for dinner, I said, "I've been thinking about Alexis. Facebook Memories reminded me it's been four years since she passed."

She replied, "I've been thinking a lot about Alexis, too. In fact, I've been sensing messages from her. She wants me to give you a stack of letters she wrote to me in 1990."

She reached into her purse and pulled out a stack of a dozen handwritten letters, written on yellow legal paper. The energy coming from those letters made it feel as though they were on fire.

I went to my parents' home and read them. I was sure I'd find something remarkable written in there, perhaps an idea for my next career. Nope. I was barely mentioned. I did take some notes from one letter, in which she said, "I recently read a book about spirituality, and here are my takeaways... One that stood out was, 'Ask God for what you want.'"

After these three conversations, I called my good friend who is a Catholic priest. I told him about these three unusual encounters and asked him what I should make of it all. He said, "I think God is trying to talk to you. You should consider an eight-day spiritual retreat with the Jesuits to discern what it means."

If I had still been working full-time at my company, I would have never taken eight days off work for a spiritual retreat. I looked online and found many options across the country. The first opening was at the Jesuit Center for Spiritual Growth in Wernersville, Pennsylvania, so I reserved a spot. I read that it was a silent retreat, but I thought that was optional. Wrong! No phone, no TV, no social media, no talking, even at meals in the cafeteria with forty other retreat participants.

I began daily spiritual direction with a Jesuit Brother, who taught me about Ignatian contemplative prayer, or "praying with imagination." I've always had a creative imagination. I made an improvised altar out of cereal boxes, remember? And I also used to enjoy pretending I was one of the paramedics on the 1970s TV show *Emergency!*

In the lovely Pennsylvanian countryside I would wander the 400-acre grounds to meditate and pray. I reflected on certain Gospels by imagining myself there, in the scene of the biblical story. After forty-five minutes of meditating, I would journal what I saw, felt, or heard. I shared the unusual encounters I'd been having with my spiritual director. I also told him about Alexis' letters. He asked me what notes I had taken from her letters. When I read off the list of bullets she wrote after reading a book on spirituality, his eyes got big when I mentioned, "Ask God for what you want."

He said, "You haven't studied Ignatian spirituality yet, but this is one of the primary tenets."

*Wow,* I thought. *Maybe Alexis wanted me to be at that spiritual retreat.*

Midway through the week, I signed up to receive a massage from a local massage therapist who came to the center from the nearby town. I laid facedown on the table and drifted in and out of sleep. A poster in the hallway read, "Pay attention to your daydreams as a way to talk with God." I liked that.

I remember the therapist rubbing my upper back and shoulders in circles. Just then, I had a vision. There were letters appearing, as if written on a whiteboard. They came in slowly, one at a time: i-m-m-i-g-r-a-n-t.

*What was that?* I thought.

*Immigrant.*

My mind was racing. I wanted to tell someone about this strange experience, especially since I'd never had a vision before. But it was a silent retreat. I had to wait until the next day to speak with my spiritual director.

When I asked him what it meant he said, "I don't know, but you're going to pray about it to find the answer." My meditation and prayer wasn't providing immediate answers, so I went on a hike along a nearby creek, while listening to music on my headphones. Nature and music have always been two things in life that help me return my mind to what's really important.

At the end of my retreat, I was using contemplative prayer to ask God for help. Should I continue focusing my passion on the environment, or should I switch to promoting kindness to strangers, immigrants, and refugees?

Within my meditative prayer, into my subconscious came two words. *Of course.*

I interpreted that to mean of course I should switch my passion, either in advocacy or as a career. After further meditation, I considered I may have a calling to use my environmental expertise to work for climate refugees. According to Refugees International, "each year millions of people are driven from their homes by floods, storms, droughts, or other weather-related disasters."

Months later, I was in New York City to bring Todd, my friend in Amsterdam whom I reached by phone on 9/11, to see *Come From Away*. I was encouraged to visit the priest at St. Francis Xavier, a Jesuit parish in Manhattan. When the taxi pulled up, I opened the door and directly in my line of sight was a huge banner that read, WELCOME IMMIGRANTS AND REFUGEES. I immediately wondered if this banner was a spiritual sign meant for me.

During Mass, I had another spiritual encounter. I felt like I was intoxicated again, though I was sober. In my prayer, I asked God, "Is this church supposed to be my spiritual home?" And again, from my subconscious mind, I felt a very strong YES!

I'd always said that though I loved to visit Manhattan, I would never live there. Those feelings changed during that one-hour Mass. Two days later, I rented an apartment and I moved to New York City a few weeks after that. I selected this apartment because it has a water view of Upper New York Bay, the waterway which led ships on the final mile of their transatlantic voyage to America. These ships carried more than 12 million immigrants to Ellis Island's immigrant inspection station between 1892 and 1954. After settling in New York, I started searching for work opportunities with immigrant and refugee agencies, and volunteering with outreach groups for LGBT Catholics and a peace and justice committee.

Alexis lived in lower Manhattan on September 11th. She had worked late the night before, so she somehow slept through all the chaos of fire truck sirens that morning. She had turned her telephone ringer and answering machine off so she could sleep late, much to the dismay of her worried family and friends. Something tells me that Alexis has been guiding me to find my next chapter in New York City.

After my spiritual awakening, I've felt as if I were flowing safely down a river. I'm not always sure of the destination, but I know I'm headed in the right direction.

*WHERE THERE'S DESPAIR in life, let us bring hope.* Back in 2005, Hurricane Katrina hit Louisiana and created hundreds of thousands of refugees, especially from New Orleans. My hometown of Austin welcomed more than four thousand of these refugees whose homes were flooded. In Gander-like fashion, Austinites donated food, clothing, and shelter to those who were living in the Austin Convention Center. Many people helped New Orleans families who had lost everything settle in Austin. That year, the sole focus for our Pay It Forward 9/11 efforts was to help the hurricane refugees. I also volunteered at the civic auditorium to help those with medical needs.

I'll never forget meeting eighty-year-old Lysle within a few minutes of arriving at the shelter. As he was exiting the bathroom, I simply asked him how he was doing, expecting him to say he was okay. Instead, he said, "Not so well. I can't find my wife."

I asked him to sit down in the cafeteria so I could learn more. Lysle's wife had cancer, and she had been staying at Mercy Hospital in New Orleans when the floodwater required all patients to be evacuated by helicopter. Unfortunately, that meant loved ones were on their own. Lysle was sent to the New Orleans Convention Center, which was hardly functioning as a working shelter. Toilets weren't working, and power was intermittent. When Lysle went to sleep that night, he took out his hearing aids and laid them on his one suitcase. Sadly, someone stole the suitcase and hearing aids while he slept. Eventually he was rescued by the National Guard and put on a flight to Austin. When he landed, he thought he was in San Antonio. This reminded me of when I was stranded in Newfoundland, when I first thought I was in Nova Scotia.

Taking Gander-like inspiration, I took on the job of a social worker, trying to help him get information about his wife and connect him to his relatives. All Lysle knew was that his wife was being medevacked to a hospital in Baton Rouge. That was enough for me to start with. After finding the phone number for hospitals in the city, I called and asked if his wife had been admitted from New Orleans. I got lucky on the first try. After a few minutes of explaining who I was, a nurse put his wife on the line, and then I handed my cell phone to Lysle. He started to cry when he heard his wife's voice. It had been five days since they last spoke. She hadn't known where he was, or if he was alive.

His wife reminded Lysle that he had a relative who lived in Austin. They gave me his name, so I called 411 information and was lucky enough to reach him by phone within minutes. I told him his great-uncle from New Orleans had been sent to the Austin refugee shelter. He told me that his relatives were all worried about him, not knowing where he had been sent. Within an hour, a young man had arrived at the shelter, ready to take Lysle to his apartment. The next day, I called a hearing aid company, telling them the story of Lysle and his stolen hearing aids. They said they would happily help him out by donating a new set to him. Weeks later, Lysle's wife was discharged from the hospital. Their New Orleans home was still off limits from the flood, so she came to live with Lysle in Austin for a few weeks. I was blessed to be able to witness their emotional reunion.

Americans are truly great at helping neighbors and strangers when there is a natural disaster. We need this same type of compassion year-round. Too often we let fear get in the way.

There's a way in which the plane people or come from aways stranded in Gander were temporary refugees of war. A war begun by Osama bin Laden had broken out in New York, Pennsylvania, and Washington, D.C. We had no information and didn't know what was going on. We just knew we needed food, clothing, and shelter. Canadian authorities could have treated the stranded passengers as refugees with terrorists among us, leaving us on the planes for days, perhaps sending out food and water. But they didn't. Every person in Gander and the surrounding towns took a chance and offered us kindness and goodwill even though they didn't have to. They let us off the planes and took care of us in the most beautiful, loving ways.

In 2016, I asked Gander mayor Claude Elliott whether they had been nervous about the risk of permitting a terrorist from one of the planes to enter their community when they helped us on that tragic day.

"I don't think we can live our life in fear. Not everybody is out to do bad things. We have to realize that not every Muslim is a terrorist. Of course there are bad people out there, but we were willing to take that chance. We weren't going to let people suffer on those planes for four to five days. That never came into our minds. Even though we've received thousands of accolades, that's not why we did it. We just say thank you and that we were paid in full by knowing we helped people at a very difficult time."

Ganderite Diane Davis echoes Mayor Elliott's sentiment. "We had passengers from all over the world, but we had no conflicts or trouble," she says. "Fear and misunderstanding lead to extreme action, but they can also lead to empathy."

About the diverse crowd of plane people from many backgrounds, Mac Moss observed: "Our passengers were wonderful. Not once did any of them try to gain advantage or preferential treatment because of their social position or station in life. No one complained about the food. A number of my teaching staff spoke French, one spoke Spanish, and one, with the aid of an electronic translator, communicated with a group that spoke Yugoslavian. Other than that we got by in English. Perhaps the language of caring spoke for all of us."

AT THE SEATTLE performance of *Come From Away*, I was invited onstage for an audience question-and-answer session for those interested in staying longer after the show. Virtually everyone in the audience stuck around.

I was asked about how my perspective of Gander had changed me. I thought about how it felt to be stranded in a remote, rural community in a place I couldn't find on the map, albeit for only a few days. Those days were profound; it was then that I felt incredible acceptance and received so much kindness. I replied, "During the attacks of 9/11, stranded airline passengers became temporary refugees. The Canadians didn't have to let us off the planes, but they did. Why is there so much hysteria about helping others in our country today, especially millions of Syrian war refugees?"

According to the United States Department of State, the United States admitted 12,500 Syrian refugees out of the five million who fled their country due to the ongoing civil war.

By November 2016, the Canadian government had already resettled 44,000 Syrian refugees. I was not surprised to learn the town of Gander was again acting as a role model for compassion and empathy, this time with Syrian refugees.

It was the unforgettable photo of Alan Kurdi, the young Syrian boy whose lifeless body washed up on a shore in Turkey, that galvanized people in Gander to step up and help refugees once again. Gander's town council organized a meeting that drew more than forty people, some of whom then formed the Gander Refugee Outreach Committee.

Mayor Elliott said, "We figured opponents would show up to the meetings, but we have not had one individual with a negative view. It's only people wanting to help. We had no major objections to bringing Syrian refugees to Gander from anyone in the community. Everyone believed that if you brought in a family, we had little to fear."

When the towns of Gander and Lewisporte decided to adopt five Syrian families, the Canadian government required that they raise $15,000 per family to receive federal funds to assist the families.

Diane Davis retired from teaching and has become a full-time volunteer for Gander Refugee Outreach. Just as she did for the 9/11 come from aways, Diane is doing anything and everything she can to help the Syrian refugees resettle in Gander. She helps co-ordinate volunteers, solicit supplies, arrange for medical care, and explain Gander culture.

Diane spoke of how challenging it was to raise money for the effort.

"There was no single donor who could write a check. The Anglican Church was first in raising funds through bake sales and other small fund-raisers. The United Church was next in raising money for the second family. Each of these churches had other fund-raising needs, like paying for roof repair on the church." She added, "But they prioritized the families in need."

Because Gander is a small, rural town, there's a shortage of physicians. One doctor, originally from Syria, commutes to Gander to help. He happened to be on a plane with the second of five Syrian refugee families that were being welcomed in Gander.

When they arrived in the Gander International Airport terminal, he witnessed an outpouring of love similar to what I saw on 9/11. The terminal was filled with people, including dozens of children, who came to welcome their new residents.

He told CBC Television, "The first thing we saw was their little child come out...he was stunned to see all these people at two in the morning." He added, "The waiting children rushed toward the boy in welcome, as the rest of the family appeared and began to cry."

The Syrian-Canadian doctor was moved. He went on, "Here I'm helping Gander, and here Gander is helping people of the same heritage as me."

Having worked closely with the families for one year now, Diane knows a lot about Syrian refugees. She believes if more people looked at refugees as individuals and families, not statistics, they might see that we are more the same than we are different. "We both like to cook and to feed people. We both want our kids to get an education. We both want to work to support our families. If we get hurt, we cry. If we get cut, we bleed. If we tell a joke, we laugh."

One of the Muslim refugees told Diane she was impressed how the Christian church volunteers practiced their religion through good deeds rather than just words. Diane says these new Canadian residents have one year of funding from the Canadian government to find work to support their families.

The refugees want to succeed, to live without social services from the government. Right away, they have done everything from cleaning dishes at a restaurant to mowing lawns. They want to be able to volunteer in their communities to help others. They want to pay it forward.

According to Refugees International, the number of displaced persons forced from their homes globally has risen from twenty-five million to sixty-five million people from 2011 to 2015. This is a crisis that goes beyond the Syrian civil war. Thousands of people are being displaced across the globe because of changes in climate and related inability to work. When tremendous floods or droughts hit a country, it's impossible for farmers to provide for their families. They may migrate within their country to a suburban area, but then they face the challenge of finding jobs that aren't in agriculture. It's a safe bet that almost all of these refugees aren't as fortunate as we were when we were stranded in Gander. Many live in tents without running water, food, or healthcare. These challenges aren't going away. In fact, if we don't sufficiently deal with the underlying causes of forced displacement, we could see more wars, more refugees, and less peace.

The kindness of strangers in Gander inspired me in 2001 and again in 2016. Being kind to strangers wasn't a one-time act for Gander. The town continues to welcome anyone and everyone, at a time when others live in fear and keep their doors closed. My faith in God and all humanity is stronger because of my experiences with Gander. Now it's my turn to champion the cause of immigrants and refugees. I have embraced my role as a channel of peace.

*Where there's despair in life, let me bring hope; Where there is darkness, only light; And where there's sadness, ever joy.* The famous "Golden Rule" from the Christian Bible, "Do unto others as you would have them do unto you" (Matthew 7:12) has almost identical teachings in Buddhism, Hinduism, Judaism, and Islam. My prayer is that as countries across the globe, we can work to better understand how much we have in common. Differences in gender, race, religion, political party, or sexual orientation shouldn't draw battle lines between the human race. We need each other to coexist in peace.

# CHAPTER 10

## No Thanks Are Necessary

ON THE FIFTEENTH anniversary of the 9/11 attacks, some American communities were dialing back the 9/11 commemorations, but the leaders at Ford's Theatre in Washington, D.C., believed *Come From Away* was exactly what their audience needed to see right then — it was needed all the more because of the political divisions.

It was surreal to find myself sitting near the front row of this historic theater, the place where President Abraham Lincoln was assassinated. The presidential box seats are empty, with a framed portrait of President George Washington facing the stage. Ford's Theatre celebrates the legacy of President Lincoln and explores the American experience through theater and education.

Before the show began, I was introduced, along with a handful of others whose stories are portrayed in the musical. I had seen the show three times already, but the anniversary and the venue, not to mention the high-profile audience members, together were really driving home the significance of this story. I thought, *Is this really happening?*

As I looked around the theater, I couldn't believe I was sitting amid some of the most high-profile political leaders in the country. Directly in front of me was Andrew Card, the chief of staff to President George W. Bush. He's the man who whispered to President Bush that America was under attack as the president read to schoolchildren in Florida. Sitting in the front row was the United States Secretary of the Interior Sally Jewell, appointed by President Obama. Behind me was Republican Senator Roy Blunt from Missouri. Across the aisle were Senators Susan Collins, a Republican from Maine, and former Senate Majority Leader Harry Reid, a Democrat from Nevada.

Since I practically knew the show by heart, I decided to watch instead how these political leaders from both parties reacted to the drama onstage. Guess what? They all laughed and cried throughout the entire performance. It didn't matter what political party you were in, this show was uniting people, reminding everyone of the power, beauty, and importance of kindness to strangers. After the show, I shook hands with Andrew Card and thanked him for his service on that tragic day. I disagreed with the decisions of Mr. Card and President Bush, taking our country into war in Iraq. Perhaps this show could unite us all back to a time of peace.

At a reception at the Canadian Embassy in Washington, D.C., David MacNaughton, the Canadian ambassador to the United States, told the guests and patrons from Ford's Theatre that "on that tragic day, Canadians lent a hand to their neighbor. No thanks are necessary. The debt is paid in full."

Mayor Claude Elliott added, "We just do good deeds and cherish the memories."

The morning after, I woke up to see a newspaper slipped underneath my hotel room door. On the front page of the Metro section of the *Washington Post* was the headline "Stranded on 9/11, a small town in Canada showed him kindness. This is how he pays it forward." The article was written by Colby Itkowitz, the *Inspired Life* blog writer for the *Post*. The writer described how I'd been true to remembering the anniversary of the attacks by encouraging kindness to strangers, and high-lighted some generous actions the cast and crew of the musical had taken the previous day.

A high-profile performance in the nation's capital was exciting, but then, a month later, I was invited by the show's producers to join the cast and crew for another special show: a benefit performance in Gander!

It's not an easy trip to get to Gander because there are no direct flights from America. I met up with a group of eighty people at LaGuardia Airport for a long day's journey, flying northwest to Toronto, then east to St. John's, Newfoundland. From there, it was a late-night four-hour bus ride to the town of Gander.

I'll never forget my 2016 Gander trip. I was again reunited with friends who had been my 9/11 caretakers. At the Gander airport, I also met Bruce Heyman, the American ambassador to Canada. He presented a beautiful bronze plaque, offering gratitude on behalf of the United States to the people of Gander and the surrounding towns for the role they played in taking care of the more than 6,500 stranded airline passengers for up to five days.

The actors, musicians, and crew were all nervous about performing the show for Gander's residents. They wanted to be sure they were 100 percent authentic with the story, the sentiment, and the Newfoundland accents.

Mayor Elliott shut down the town's hockey rink (that's huge!) to accommodate 2,500 people for each of the two performances. Roughly half of the town saw the musical in Gander that day, and they absolutely loved it. They cheered, laughed, cried, sang, and danced throughout. It was the blessing that everyone related to the show was looking for before going on to runs in Toronto and on Broadway.

For the opening night on Broadway on March 12, 2017, the producers generously brought all the doppelgängers portrayed in the show to New York City. It was great to see my friends from Gander. My ex-partner Evan was there too, and we shook hands and talked for the first time in more than seven years. Then we all joined the actors who were portraying us and walked out onstage during the curtain call. Although we hadn't sung a note or danced, we were told to take a bow before a rousing standing ovation. It was an unforgettable moment.

On June 11, 2017, *Come From Away* won a Tony Award from the American Theatre Wing for Best Direction of a Musical. The show was nominated for seven awards, including Best Musical. Director Christopher Ashley was recognized for his remarkable ability to tell the story of the plane people and the local Newfoundlanders with just twelve actors, using only twelve chairs and two tables. I was there at Radio City Music Hall, joining Maureen Murray and Sue Riccardelli, Beverley Bass and Tom Stawicki, and Nick and Diane Marson. We were excited our story was reaching millions via the live telecast.

When I first met David and Irene, none of us knew how timely the message of *Come From Away* would soon become. I think it's not a coincidence that the musical's appeal has grown at the same time as we've seen a resurgence of talk by people of influence in the public sphere that encourages people who fear or hate foreigners or people from different cultures. Civil wars, climate change, and religious conflicts have caused the world's refugee crisis to grow, and people are struggling with how to handle strangers in need arriving upon their doorsteps and at the borders.

This story of showing kindness to strangers is resonating with audiences so much that it continues to sell out tickets on a nightly basis, including standing room only tickets. Producers from Junkyard Dog Productions announced they recouped their $12 million investment in less than eight months on Broadway. Plans were announced for a new Canadian cast to perform shows in Winnipeg and Toronto in 2018. Also, a North American touring company is planned for 2018–2019.

In mid-2017, HBO Canada agreed to produce *You Are Here*, a documentary about the making of *Come From Away*. Director Moze Mossanen called to invite me on a return trip to Gander for a reunion of the real people who inspired the characters in the musical. I never turn down an opportunity to return to Newfoundland, so I agreed. Evan also decided to go, and it was his first return visit to Gander. We hadn't talked at all since the opening night on Broadway, and before that, it had been seven years since we had spoken. It was both awkward and easy to be around each other.

We conducted a joint interview, and then I drove Evan around Gander in a special van which was recording on video all our conversations. We visited Mac and

Nellie Moss, who joined our discussions for the documentary in their backyard with Little Cobb's Pond in the background. Evan was a good sport, agreeing to be screeched in as an honorary Newfoundlander at a fundraiser for the Gander SPCA. Mayor Claude Elliott did the honor, in front of one hundred locals. I was happy Evan could return and enjoy Gander in ways we didn't when we were 9/11 refugees in 2001.

Imagine if you received an email saying your personal story, now being told in a hit musical, will soon become a Hollywood movie. In November 2017, Marc Gordon announced he would produce *Come From Away* as a feature film. Gordon has produced big-screen hits like *Saving Private Ryan* and TV hits like *Grey's Anatomy*. Everyone hopes to film on location, starting at Gander International Airport. David Hein and Irene Sankoff have been named screenwriters, and Christopher Ashley will be the director.

THOUSANDS OF PEOPLE now know the story of what happened in Gander on those transformative days. When I reflect on them now, Mac Moss's words come to mind: "Every day of our lives we get an opportunity to practice the Golden Rule, 'Do unto others as you would have them do unto you.' Only once in a lifetime does an opportunity come along to practice this rule on such a grand scale." It is my hope that we all find ways every day to feel a deep sense of connection and acceptance, show kindness by doing good deeds even for strangers, and keep hope alive by supporting public policy that provides help for immigrants and refugees.

You never know if or when you may find yourself as the stranger in a strange land. As they sing in the musical, "because we come from everywhere, we all come from away."

Consider putting down your electronic devices once in a while and looking up at strangers to truly see them. As Mayor Elliott said, "Love, compassion, and understanding: that is what the world is lacking today. If Gander's story can help someone, then we need to tell it over and over again." Love is the motivation for kindness. Not the romantic or familial love that we all know, but rather a love for humanity. After all, isn't that what we're here for?

# APPENDIX

## Ten Ways to Pay It Forward

PEOPLE CAN BE nervous about approaching strangers to do a good deed as a random act of kindness. You might try it any day of the year, but September 11th is a good one. In 2009, former president Barack Obama declared it the National Day of Service and Remembrance and in 2011 Canada followed suit.

One easy way to start a conversation with a stranger is to say, "Hello, today is the anniversary of the September 11th attacks, and I'm part of a group doing good deeds to honor the lives lost and heroes who helped others on 9/11. I'd like to give you _____, and if you'd like to, you might continue the movement by doing the same for another stranger you meet."

Now you know what to say, but perhaps you need ideas on what and where you might get started. You'll be surprised how quickly the ripple effect begins as the recipient starts to think about how they can pay it forward. Here are a few ideas.

## 1. THANK FIRST RESPONDERS

Many people show their appreciation for police, fire, and EMS workers on the anniversary of 9/11 because so many were lost in rescue efforts at the World Trade Center. Our EnviroMedia staff frequently visited a fire or police station, offering various gifts, usually food.

In Portland, Oregon, one team visited the administrative office of a fire department—people who are often overlooked—and provided them with a free lunch. Breakfast tacos were delivered one year to new firefighter cadets who were in the middle of training to climb the stairwells of tall buildings carrying heavy equipment.

One way to thank first responders, which only costs the price of a postage stamp, is to write thank-you notes to military, police, fire, and EMS personnel. In Nashville, one teacher made this part of a civics lesson, assigning each seventh-grader to write these letters, which were then mailed by the school to nearby offices.

## 2. HEAD TO THE HOSPITAL

Over the years, several Pay It Forward teams have gone to hospitals to perform random acts of kindness. In the maternity ward, savings bonds were given in the names of newborns born on September 11th, so their birthday would be remembered in a positive way — as often these gifts are 9/11 memorials. One employee went to a hospital, explained her mission, and asked where the greatest need was.

The hospital told her that there was a woman there who had lived in New York on 9/11. She was a grandmother raising the child of a parent who died in the World Trade Center. The grandmother cried tears of joy after accepting a cash gift and a card. She said that she would continue the effort by paying it forward to someone else. Another staffer went to the cancer ward and gave some money to a woman waiting for chemotherapy treatment.

## 3. FIND OUT WHAT YOUR LOCAL SCHOOL NEEDS

Usually it just takes one quick phone call to a school principal to find someone who would appreciate a hundred-dollar gift. At one school, two low-income kids recently had their bicycles stolen. The parents couldn't afford to replace them, and the kids had to walk a long distance to school. Two bikes were delivered that day.

Another elementary school principal explained that the school had installed a new garden, but they needed gardening tools. Rakes, shovels, hoes, and gloves were purchased and delivered that day.

A similar request for help in the garden came from a different school, which really needed mulch fertilizer. The principal arranged for nearly three hundred kids to assemble outside at the garden. After explaining to the children about the importance of remembering those who died on 9/11, and the story of Gander's kindness, our employee pulled out a hundred-dollar bill and explained that one child would receive this money to use for their own Pay It Forward 9/11 good deed. Several kids shared their ideas for helping others, and one was chosen to receive the prize.

But that wasn't all! Using their own money, one of my teams had arranged to purchase a dump-truck-full of mulch for the school garden. On cue, they yelled, "Bring on the mulch!" The truck pulled around and dumped the mulch at the garden site. The kids went wild, screaming with delight...over *mulch*! A teacher told our team, "I saw a story on the news about this effort, and I said to myself, I wish that would happen to my school. And it did!"

## 4. OFFER A SIMPLE CUP OF COFFEE

Since the *Pay It Forward* movie, many news stories have been written about random good deeds.

There was a news story of a Starbucks in Florida at which a woman gave additional money to the cashier, telling them to pay for the coffee of the person behind her in line. That person was so surprised, they said, "I'll keep it going, use my money to pay for the person behind me." And it kept on going, and going, and going for eleven hours. In the end, 378 people had paid for a stranger's coffee.

During our Pay It Forward 9/11 events, many people visited coffee shops or food trucks to plunk down $20 or more to pay for coffees or sandwiches ordered by the next random customers. Sometimes, our staffers would explain; other times, they would sit back and watch the reactions of people after they had their coffee or sandwich paid for by a stranger. A smile bloomed on each customer's face, every time. One of our staffers purchased a Starbucks gift card and put $50 on it. They gave it to a random customer and told them to pay for someone else's coffee, and to invite that person to continue doing the same, until the card ran out of money.

Eight months later, I received a phone call from a nonprofit executive who was familiar with our company and our annual tradition. She said, "You won't believe what happened to me today. I was meeting a potential new donor for coffee. When I went to purchase it, the person I was meeting with handed me a Starbucks gift card. The woman said, 'Oh, I'm supposed to buy your coffee using this gift card. It's some sort of pay it forward thing.' I told her, 'I know where this came from. It started months ago on September 11th.'

My guess is that people added money to the card when the balance went low, which kept the free coffees flowing for months."

## 5. LOOK FOR IDEAS IN THE CRAIGSLIST "WANTED" SECTION

One team searched Craigslist and found an ad about a battered woman living in a women's shelter after leaving a twenty-year abusive relationship. She had nothing. She was using a Thomas the Train comforter for her bed. So they bought her a nice, new comforter. They also bought her beauty and bath products to pamper herself. On Craigslist, I searched the term "wanted" under the General Community section. I found that some people had simple requests like a ride across town. Another post, titled "In desperate need," was a person who lost his job unexpectedly and needed help purchasing Christmas presents for his son. This person wrote, "I am at the point where I don't know what to do and don't have anywhere to turn."

Is it an online scam? I doubt it.

## 6. THANK AIRLINE INDUSTRY WORKERS

Anyone who flies in airplanes for a living or works at an airport knows there is the threat of a copycat terror attack on the anniversary of 9/11. One year, I happened to be on another international flight, traveling from Tokyo to New York. I didn't have time to purchase anything before getting on board. Thankfully, our large jumbo jet came with its own duty-free shop. I saw that they had red, white, and blue jelly beans for sale. I purchased one box for each of the twelve flight attendants and wrote a note explaining why I was doing this. Over the course of the flight, each of the flight attendants came by my seat to personally thank me for thinking of them in this way.

One staffer thought a lot about flight crews and thanking them for their service on the anniversary. Back in 2002, before the widespread popularity of cell phones, most pilots used long-distance calling cards. She bought and distributed these cards to several pilots in uniform as they arrived at the airport. She once provided snacks to cashiers who worked at airport parking lot toll booths. Another year, she contacted the director of Austin's FAA air traffic control tower and explained that she wanted to bring a cake to the controllers on duty that day.

## 7. GIVE AWAY FLOWERS TO BRIGHTEN SOMEONE'S DAY

At the famous Pike Place Market in Seattle, one team purchased dozens of daisies and proceeded to hand them out one by one to random shoppers, along with a small note card that read, "Smile. You're the recipient of a random act of kindness." There were dozens of smiles in the market that day. In Portland, one team went to a local florist and picked up the tab for a man buying roses for his girlfriend. He was touched and pledged to pay it forward.

## 8. HELP SOCIAL SERVICE AGENCIES

Many groups have supported a local battered women's shelter, a refugee outreach group, a foster home, a teen drug and alcohol rehabilitation center, a hospice, or a food bank. After you decide which agency to support, call in advance and ask for a manager. Explain what you're trying to do and ask what items they might need. Often, they need simple items and the money for them just isn't in their budget. One teen rehab center wanted colored pencils and candy. A Ronald McDonald House temporary residence for the parents of children in the hospital needed detergent for its washing machine. A hospice wanted current magazines for loved ones visiting patients to read in the lobby. A homeless shelter wanted men's white tube socks. A VA hospital wanted transit passes to help low-income veterans get to their appointments. A blood bank—well, you know what they needed.

## 9. FEED THE METER OR THE VENDING MACHINE

In cities that still have parking meters that require coins, it's easy to add a quarter or more to someone's parking meter when it has expired or is about to expire.

Many of our staff did this over the years. Most likely you won't get the opportunity to witness the recipient's reaction to this good deed. They may not even realize they were at risk of getting a parking ticket. You might add a note to the windshield explaining the concept of Pay It Forward. One person went further, going to traffic court to pay for the parking tickets of strangers.

Be creative! There are lots of transportation-related deeds you can do. Anyone waiting at a bus shelter or subway station would appreciate a free transit pass.

Sometimes we provided free snacks or candy to college students by taping dollar bills to the front of vending machines on campus.

## 10. DO SOMETHING THAT BRINGS YOU GREAT JOY

There are countless opportunities to bring joy to others through a random act of kindness. They don't have to cost money, but a small donation can go a long way. If you've never tried doing random acts of kindness, but you want to, put some thought into something that really connects with you. Did someone or some organization help you along the way at some point in your life?

In 2000, Shelly received the gift of life from a random stranger: a new kidney from an anonymous organ donor. She had been diagnosed with diabetes at twenty and she was set to receive a kidney donated by her father, but when it came time for his surgery doctors found that his kidney had cancer. Her father was successfully treated for cancer, and Shelly received the beautiful gift of a new kidney from an organ donor, a stranger who died unexpectedly. In 2005, Shelly contributed her company Pay It Forward donation to the Texas Renal Coalition, a local kidney healthcare organization. She has served the organization ever since. More importantly, she used her time at the post-event staff meeting to explain the importance of organ donation. She also passed out printed information about the Donate Life campaign to staff members, encouraging them to become organ donors. Her story moved me and others to sign up with the organ donor registry.

One staffer decided he wanted to do something nice for his childhood cello instructor. He felt his life was changed by learning and appreciating music. On September 11th, he showed up at the music school and found his same instructor, still teaching after twenty years. He donated money to the school so that a low-income student could receive a few music lessons from that instructor. Tears were shed. Joy happened. Kindness was spread to a stranger.

THERE ARE MANY organizations, including 911Day.org and DayofService.ca, that offer ideas and resources to participate. "Never forget" must be more than a social media hashtag. Consider some act of personal or community service on the next anniversary, and remember you can do a good deed for a stranger any day of the year.

## ACKNOWLEDGEMENTS

I THANK GOD for giving me an amazing family, especially my parents, James and Julie Tuerff. Their unwavering love and support has been a source of constant encouragement. I also appreciate the encouragement of my three brothers and their families: Brian and Jana Tuerff; Jeff and Lynn Tuerff; Greg and Jayne Tuerff; and eight remarkable nieces and nephews — Alison, Brenna, Breann, Parker, Travis, Amanda, Kelly, and Connor.

In my career, I'm grateful for everyone at EnviroMedia who helped Valerie Salinas-Davis and me create and grow that business. Their loyalty and hard work allowed us to help clients improve public health and the environment while finding ways to demonstrate our commitment to philanthropic efforts like Pay It Forward 9/11. I'm grateful to Catherine Ryan Hyde for writing *Pay It Forward* and starting a foundation to encourage random acts of kindness.

I am grateful to these friends for their help and support with this book: Mark Aitala and Sara Beechner, Maureen Basnicki, Kevin Burns, Diane Davis, Claude Elliott, Dan and Melanie Fish, Sue Frost, Rebecca Geier, David Hein and Irene Sankoff, Bill House, Kitten Howard, Chad Kimball, Margaret Lee, John Markey, O.P., Nick and Diane Marson, Mac and Nellie Moss, Maureen Murray and Sue Riccardelli, Sean Price, Michael Rubinoff, Todd Savage, Michael Staffieri, Tom Stawicki and Beverly Bass, Brett Will Taylor, and Ron and Sue Walsh.

I am also grateful for my publishing teams, including Hobbs Allison, April Jo Murphy, Daniel Pederson, and Brian Phillips at River Grove Books and Greenleaf Book Group, and Sarah MacLachlan, Janie Yoon, Michelle MacAleese, Maria Golikova, Sara Loos, and Alysia Shewchuk at House of Anansi Press.

Author photograph: Devaki Knowles

**KEVIN TUERFF** is a social entrepreneur, speaker, and author with over twenty-five years of experience in marketing and public affairs. He is the CEO of Kevin Tuerff Consulting, LLC, a public relations and marketing practice. He is also an Ambassador for the Charter of Compassion.

In 1997, Tuerff cofounded EnviroMedia, the first integrated marketing agency dedicated solely to improving public health and the environment. When he was president, he cofounded America Recycles Day and helped Daimler launch an innovative carsharing service across North America. He also helped the State of Texas prevent death and disease through public health behavior change campaigns.

For more than fifteen years, he has organized a kindness initiative to commemorate the anniversary of September 11, 2001, called Pay It Forward 9/11.

Tuerff is passionate about the planet and its people, donating time to a number of organizations that support the cause. For four years, he was an elected director of a water utility, where he championed water conservation programs during an extreme drought. In 2016, he received an outstanding leadership award from the University of Texas Environmental Science Institute for his eight years of volunteer service, and in 2017, a Distinguished Alumnus Award from the Friar Society at the University of Texas.

A resident of Austin for over thirty years, Tuerff now lives in New York City. He is an active member of St. Francis Xavier Catholic Church.

You can follow Kevin on
- Facebook.com/ChannelofPeaceGander
- Twitter @channelof_peace
- Instagram @channel_of_peace_book.